THE HERMENEUTICS OF LIFE HISTORY

Northwestern University
Studies in Phenomenology
and
Existential Philosophy

THE HERMENEUTICS OF LIFE HISTORY

Personal Achievement and History in Gadamer, Habermas, and Erikson

Jerald Wallulis

Northwestern University Press
Evanston, Illinois

Northwestern University Press
Evanston, Illinois 60201

Copyright © 1990 by Northwestern University Press
All rights reserved. First published 1990
Printed in the United States of America

95 94 93 92 91 90   5 4 3 2 1

Library of Congress Cataloging-in-Publication Data

Wallulis, Jerald, 1947–
    The hermeneutics of life history : personal achievement and
history in Gadamer, Habermas, and Erikson / Jerald Wallulis.
        p.   cm.—(Northwestern University studies in phenomenology
and existential philosophy)
    Includes bibliographical references and index.
    ISBN 0-8101-0967-0 (alk. paper)
    1. Hermeneutics. 2. Biography. 3. Psychoanalysis and philosophy.
4. Gadamer, Hans Georg, 1900–   . 5. Habermas, Jürgen. 6. Erikson,
Erik H. (Erik Homburger), 1902–   . I. Title. II. Title: Personal
achievement and history in Gadamer, Habermas, and Erikson.
III. Series: Northwestern University studies in phenomenology &
existential philosophy.
BD241.W343   1990
128'.5—dc20
                                                            90-49019
                                                            CIP

To my parents

Contents

Acknowledgments

In a book where the concept of enablement plays a very prominent role, there are many enablements to be acknowledged. Material on Habermas from the second chapter was originally worked on in my dissertation, and I acknowledge Gary Gutting and Fabio Dasilva for their assistance. The dissertation project itself was made possible through an intervention by Richard Bernstein, which allowed me to have contact with Jürgen Habermas who helped me understand the chapters on psychoanalysis in *Knowledge and Human Interests*. My knowledge of Habermas's thought and of the philosophical hermeneutics of Gadamer were also greatly furthered by my participation in an NEH summer seminar directed by Thomas McCarthy. The idea for the book project itself developed out of another NEH summer offering, an institute directed by Calvin Schrag. Both directors have continued to assist me in the development of the project, with Professor Schrag playing an especially encouraging role.

Others who have read a preliminary draft of the manuscript and made very useful comments include Joel Weinsheimer, David Ingram, and, above all, the readers commissioned by the Northwestern University Press—Tom Rockmore, David M. Levin, and Merold Westphal. Paul Ricoeur also aided me at a much earlier stage in understanding his position more clearly. At my own institution, the University of South Carolina, Eve Tavor Bannet, Gene Long, Martin Donougho, and Davis Baird have also offered their advice. Finally, two very different forms of enablement need to be mentioned: first, the philosophy department and College of Humanities and Social Sciences of the University of South Carolina for financially supporting my sabbatical study in the spring of 1987; and second, my wife and daughter for the human support they have continually provided.

The following publishers have generously given permission to use extended quotations from copyrighted works: From *Philosophical Hermeneutics* by Hans-Georg Gadamer, edited and translated by David Linge. Copyright 1976 by The Regents of the University of California. Reprinted by permission of the University of California Press. From *Truth and Method* by Hans-Georg Gadamer, edited by Garrett Barden and John Cumming. Copyright 1975 by The Continuum Publishing Company. Reprinted by permission of the publisher. From *The Theory of Communicative Action. Volume Two. Lifeworld and System: A Critique of Functionalist Reason* by Jürgen Habermas, translated by Thomas McCarthy. Copyright 1987 by Beacon Press (English translation), German copyright 1981 by Suhrkamp Verlag, Frankfurt. Reprinted by permission of Beacon Press. From *The Critical Theory of Jürgen Habermas* by Thomas McCarthy. Copyright 1978 by MIT Press. Reprinted by permission of the publisher. From *Gadamer's Hermeneutics: A Reading of Truth and Method* by Joel C. Weinsheimer. Copyright 1985 by Yale University Press. Reprinted by permission of the publisher.

Suhrkamp Verlag, Frankfurt, has generously given the author permission to use his own English translations of selections from the following: *Zur Rekonstruktion des Historischen Materialismus* by Jürgen Habermas. Copyright 1976 by Suhrkamp Verlag. From *Sprachzerstörung und Rekonstruktion* by Alfred Lorenzer. Copyright 1970 by Suhrkamp Verlag.

Abbreviations

The following list is of works cited in the text and whose full bibliographical details are to be found on pp. 148–50.

AA Jerome Bruner, "The Artist as Analyst."

AV Alasdair MacIntyre, *After Virtue.*

BLC Erik Erikson, "Reflections on Dr. Borg's Life Cycle."

C&S Erik Erikson, *Childhood and Society.*

CES Jürgen Habermas, *Communication and the Evolution of Society.*

CI Paul Ricoeur, *The Conflict of Interpretations.*

CTJH Thomas McCarthy, *The Critical Theory of Jürgen Habermas.*

DV Carol Gilligan, *In a Different Voice.*

EE Robert Coles, *Erik H. Erikson.*

EI Jürgen Habermas, *Die Entwicklung des Ich.*

F&P Paul Ricoeur, *Freud and Philosophy.*

GH Joel C. Weinsheimer, *Gadamer's Hermeneutics.*

GM Donald Browning, *Generative Man.*

H&HS Paul Ricoeur, *Hermeneutics and the Human Sciences.*

H&MP Brice R. Wachterhauser, ed., *Hermeneutics and Modern Philosophy.*

HAS Jürgen Habermas, *Habermas: Autonomy & Solidarity.*

HCE Stephen White, "Habermas' Communicative Ethics and the Development of Moral Consciousness."

HDR David Ingram, *Habermas and the Dialectic of Reason.*

HW Jean Grondin, *Hermeneutische Wahrheit?*

I&LC Erik Erikson, *Identity and the Life Cycle.*

I&R Erik Erikson, *Insight and Responsibility.*

I&U Paul Ricoeur, *Lectures on Ideology and Utopia.*

IB Ingmar Bergman, *Four Screenplays of Ingmar Bergman.*

IC Clifford Geertz, "Deep Play."

IG Hans-Georg Gadamer, *The Idea of the Good in Platonic-Aristotelian Philosophy.*

IT Paul Ricoeur, *Interpretation Theory.*

IY&C Erik Erikson, *Identity: Youth and Crisis.*

K&HI Jürgen Habermas, *Knowledge and Human Interests.*

KK Jürgen Habermas, *Kultur und Kritik.*

LCC Erik Erikson, *The Life Cycle Completed.*

LHHM Erik Erikson, *Life History and the Historical Moment.*

MH Jürgen Habermas, *Moralbewusstsein und kommunikatives Handeln.*

P&ST Ian Craib, *Psychoanalysis and Social Theory.*

PDM Jürgen Habermas, *The Philosophical Discourse of Modernity.*

PH Hans-Georg Gadamer, *Philosophical Hermeneutics.*

RAS Hans-Georg Gadamer, *Reason in the Age of Science.*

RB Hans-Georg Gadamer, *The Relevance of the Beautiful and Other Essays.*

S&R Alfred Lorenzer, *Sprachzerstörung und Rekonstruktion.*

SI Jürgen Habermas, "On Social Identity."

T&M Hans-Georg Gadamer, *Truth and Method.*

T&P Jürgen Habermas, *Theory and Practice.*

T&R Erik Erikson, *Toys and Reasons.*

TCA1 Jürgen Habermas, *The Theory of Communicative Action. Volume One.*

TCA2 Jürgen Habermas, *The Theory of Communicative Action. Volume Two.*

TCC Jürgen Habermas, "Toward a Theory of Communicative Competence."

VET Jürgen Habermas, *Vorstudien und Ergänzungen zur Theorie des kommunikativen Handelns.*

W&M Hans-Georg Gadamer, *Wahrheit und Methode.*

WLT Erik Erikson, *A Way of Looking at Things.*

WP Carol Gilligan, "Woman's Place in Man's Life Cycle."

YML Erik Erikson, *Young Man Luther.*

ZLS Jürgen Habermas, *Zur Logik der Sozialwissenschaften.*

ZRHM Jürgen Habermas, *Zur Rekonstruktion des Historischen Materialismus.*

Introduction

This is a study on the topic, the sense, the consciousness, and the importance of personal achievement in relationship to life history and history in general. The topic of personal achievement has been chosen instead of subjectivity or individuality, but not in order to signal a clearly different subject matter. Rather I wish to avoid the immediate associations that are made with the highly theorized and particularized context of a philosophy of the subject or with the politically charged context of the problem of individualism. My primary concern is not with a theory of the will, of consciousness, or of individual reason, nor is it with an analysis of agency or of moral or political autonomy. Rather it is in what allows important events that happen to individuals to be correctly described at the same time as personal actions that are attributable to them. I wish to direct attention to the sense of personal achievement that is associated with these actions/events.

I seek to convey the sense of personal achievement by elucidating the significant role of personal accomplishment in the descriptions of events of individual life history. This sense of personal achievement is what is sought by the child in the desire for individual mastery evidenced by childhood play. It is what is felt necessary by the adolescent under the pressure of personal career and life decisions. Finally it is itself what is scrutinized in moments when the individual life history is personally examined and appropriated.

With respect to the consciousness of personal achievement, I am concerned with it not as the most prominent attribute of a philosophy of consciousness but rather in terms of its role in the personal appropriation and self-examination of individual life history. I wish to capture a consciousness of enablement that is quite different in its emphasis from either a consciousness of emancipation or the consciousness of being effected by history and tradition. It is a consciousness of having been enabled to achieve and of now being competent or capable to act or initiate in one's life history.

Finally, I wish to attribute to personal achievement an importance in its own right—not of course outside its historical context but also not subordinated to it either. Rather than a clear privileging of history and tradition over personal achievement, I speak of a balance of importance between them. Even more importantly, I argue for the need of avoiding in the first place an oppositional statement of the relationship between them in favor of the recognition of the complementarity between the reality of historical belongingness and the sense of personal achievement. The recognition of this complementarity and the balancing of importances between history and personal achievement can allow the subject matter of life history to become more significant—indeed more "proper"—for philosophical hermeneutics. In this way, the advocacy of the importance of personal achievement for hermeneutics is at the same time an argument for a hermeneutics of life history both distinct from and complementary to the hermeneutics of tradition and history in general.

Gadamer, Erikson, and Habermas

I have written *The Hermeneutics of Life History* in most direct philosophical relationship to the treatment of personal achievement in Hans-Georg Gadamer's *Truth and Method*. His conception of philosophical hermeneutics allows for the discussion of a broad theme like personal achievement, perhaps more so than a more

particular theory of the subject, philosophy of subjectivity, or analysis of agency. It also includes as central
elements phenomenological descriptions of play and
conversation, and an analysis of the nature and role of
consciousness. Although phenomenological description
may be out of favor in many quarters at the moment
and although the topic of the nature and role of
consciousness is often neglected or dismissed entirely,
these are for me very important resources for the
descriptions of a sense of personal achievement and of
the consciousness of enablement.

However, I do not only present Gadamer's description of play and the analysis of consciousness as they
appear in *Truth and Method*. Rather, in regard to my
theme of personal achievement, I consider another
description of play, in particular childhood play, and
develop an alternative conception of consciousness to
complement Gadamer's analysis of historical consciousness. Therefore one purpose of my study is to take the
subject matter of personal achievement as it is discussed
within the context of philosophical hermeneutics and
problematize it in terms of alternative descriptions and
analyses.

The aspect of Gadamer's treatment of personal
achievement that I most seek to make problematic
appears in the most rhetorical formulations of *Truth and
Method* concerning the limits of subjectivity and individual self-awareness. These formulations involve an
overwhelmingly favorable contrast between the importance of historical belongingness and situatedness, and
the limitations of consciousness and the role of human
will and purpose associated with a philosophy of the
subject or of consciousness or of will. In their polemical
character they are similar to other more recent critiques
in Continental thought that do not attack the theme of
personal achievement per se or relate it directly to tradition, but do write of the decentering of the subject, the
production of subjectivity, and the dissemination of
intertextuality. My hope is to address the import of at
least some of these critiques in future work, but my
present concern is to take issue with the emphasis or
one-sidedness of the comparison between history and

tradition, on the one hand, and personal achievement, on the other.

Probably the best Gadamerian examples of the priority of history over accomplishment occur in the context of his attack on the "prejudice against prejudice." For Gadamer the preunderstanding conveyed in the pre- of prejudice expresses what is prior to conscious judgment and yet what makes all conscious understanding and judgment possible. He writes of the importance of prejudice:

> In fact history does not belong to us, but we
> belong to it. Long before we understand ourselves
> through the process of self-examination, we
> understand ourselves in a self-evident way in the
> family, society and state in which we live. The
> focus of subjectivity is a distorting mirror. The
> self-awareness of the individual is only a flickering
> in the closed circuits of historical life. That is why
> the prejudices of the individual, far more than his
> judgments, constitute the historical reality of his
> being. [T&M, 245][1]

I do not seek in any way to oppose Gadamer's conception of prejudice, but only the privileging of history and prejudice over subjectivity and self-awareness. There may indeed have been historical reasons for the polemical comparison, but my belief is that the rhetorical battle against philosophies of the will, of the subject, and of consciousness has been successfully waged[2] and the continued denigration of the phenomena on which these philosophies were based is not really needed. More importantly, the most polemical statement in the quoted passage presents a considerable obstacle to any examination, let alone a philosophical hermeneutical examination, into individual self-awareness: Why even bother to investigate a "flickering in the closed circuits of historical life"? This obstacle of implied triviality is most unfortunate because philosophical hermeneutics might otherwise be able to contribute to an understanding of personal achievement not recognized and appreciated by other philosophical approaches and social scientific methods. Therefore my second goal in this study, beyond problematizing the discussion of personal achievement in *Truth and Method*, is to pursue a more positive treatment of personal achievement by seeing it and historical belongingness as complementary and not rival aspects of the same historical process.

The most important contribution I hope to make on the subject of personal achievement involves both a contrast and a parallel to an even more famous Gadamerian concept than the concept of prejudice. This concept, *wirkungsgeschichtliches Bewusstsein*, has been translated as "consciousness of effective history," but it is also translated by other authors as "consciousness in which history is ever at work" or the "consciousness of standing within a still operant history"[3] and will be translated in the new edition of *Truth and Method* as "historically effected consciousness."[4] The consciousness discloses, as all the translations indicate, the great role of effective history, but also, in a matter quite analogous to the discussion of prejudice, the limitations of consciousness. "*Wirkungsgeschichtliches Bewusstsein* is," writes Gadamer, "in an unavoidable manner more being (*Sein*) than consciousness (*Bewusstsein*)" (PH, 38). Therefore the consciousness of effective history involves the recognition that we are part of a larger effective history that happens to us beyond our willing and doing more than it is guided by our conscious direction.[5]

Unlike Gadamer, I wish to articulate another aspect or kind of consciousness in accordance with the theme of personal achievement. Rather than a consciousness of being an effect of history and tradition, it is, as stated above, a consciousness of having been enabled to achieve. Nevertheless it is intended to complement, not rival, the consciousness of having been effected. And, in this respect directly analogous to Gadamer's *wirkungsgeschichtliches Bewusstsein*, the "having been" in the consciousness of having been enabled is crucially important. It points to a prehistory of personal achievement that is just as significant as the history of achievement that follows it, to a "being" as well as to a "consciousness" of achievement. This prehistory is not, I would claim, only the results of the events of history and the preunderstanding of prejudice, but also of "pre-achievements," actions (or preactions) of an individual on the way toward the personal achievements of being an actor. The specific contributions that I seek to make concerning the subject of personal achievement are to describe the nature and role of these preachievements and to indicate how their effects on individual life history are similar in their enabling character to those of prejudices in Gadamer's conception of *Wirkungsgeschichte*.

However, in order to make these contributions, a quite different use will have to be made of the same phenomenological descriptions that are effectively and perhaps even dramatically employed to characterize the self-limiting character of *wirkungsgeschichtliches Bewusstsein*. These descriptions of play, *Bildung*, understanding, and appropriation are all characterized as events that take up or immerse their participants in their own happenings so that, in the most important description of play, the players "are played." Play, as well as the other related hermeneutical processes, will be described here above all in reference to individual mastery, of being or of being on the way toward personal achievement. Rather than Gadamer's "event structure," an "action structure" of play and appropriation is emphasized as essential for understanding the consciousness of having been enabled and for comprehending adequately the subject of personal achievement. Again the enabling aspect of the action structure is not intended as a competitor, but rather as a complement to the limiting character of the happening structure. The strategy is to describe play, *Bildung*, and appropriation as both historical events *and* personal actions, without a clear priority being assigned to either aspect.

My inspiration for undertaking these redescriptions that reflect both the importance of historical belongingness and an appreciation for personal achievement derives from the other major direct influence on the study, the psychoanalyst Erik Erikson. In a recent review of a compendium of Erikson's essays entitled *A Way of Looking at Things*, Jerome Bruner has distinguished between a "Standard Version" Erikson in step with orthodox Freudian psychoanalysis and a "literary-phenomenological" Erikson, who is the "self-styled 'phenomenologist,' the artist with an eye to life at the 'borderlines' "[6] (AA, 10). While it may seem initially disorienting or at least surprising to consider Erikson a phenomenologist, my reading of many of his essays and books accords with Bruner's that there is a "literary-phenomenological" aspect to his writings, and I feel that this aspect provides a "Way of Looking at Things" that is—or, perhaps better, needs to be made—of value to philosophical hermeneutics.

Erikson's way of looking at things is present, in my estimation, in both his historical and biographical studies and in his more "theoretical" writings as well. Indeed the more theoretical descriptions of the development and integration of ego identity in his famous eight-stage model of the life cycle are the primary influence in this study for the emphasis upon the complementarity of historical belongingness and personal achievement. However, this influence comes from an admittedly hermeneutically inspired reading of the model that comprehends it not so much as a generalized psychological theory for our and other cultures, but rather as an expression of autobiographical narration in a personalized and particularized form. The crucial elements of this reading are my attempts to incorporate Erikson's descriptions of childhood play and the social play of adolescents into the context of philosophical hermeneutical treatments of play and *Bildung*, and to explicate his description of a process of final consolidation as the deeply personal aspect of the historical process of appropriation.

The third and final goal of my project is to relate the positive results of this hermeneutical reading of Erikson on the subject matter of life history to other Continental philosophical contributions on the related topics of the subject and subjectivity. As stated in the beginning, the comparison and confrontation with more critical stances toward subjectivity is primarily a matter for future research. In this study, however, my Eriksonian-inspired discussions of personal achievement and the consciousness of enablement are related not only to the treatment of personal achievement and historical consciousness in Gadamer's philosophical hermeneutics, but also to the different theoretical treatments of self-reflection and ego identity by Jürgen Habermas. This latter relationship allows for differentiation from and comparison with a truly important contemporary "defender" of subjectivity.

To discuss Habermas's important contributions to the theory of subjectivity, it is of course also necessary to take up the Gadamer/Habermas debate. Indeed the debate has a quite prominent role in the study, both because of the Gadamer/Habermas comparison between historically effected consciousness and emancipatory self-reflection, and because of the clarification it gives to Gadamer's claim of the importance of historical situatedness. However, the study is not itself about the confrontation between philosophical hermeneutics and critical theory as global approaches to history and social theory. Insofar as I propose a conception of personal history more hermeneutical in nature, it may of course appear that I am continuing the debate. However, I would prefer to say that the lesson of the debate lies in the necessity of according value to perspectives toward history of both continuity and preservation, on the one hand, and critique and emancipation, on the other, and that I am merely applying this lesson to the further context of personal history.

My aim is to develop a different kind of philosophical hermeneutical treatment of life history, without an accompanying claim of superiority or universality as in the debate. Nevertheless I believe that it has a crucial contribution to make in the understanding of personal achievement. In comparison to Habermas, that contribution can be seen in the form of a counterthrust to the rationally reconstructive schemes of individual development. If the first treatment of self-reflection by Habermas is emancipatory in tone and this tone continues in later theories of ego identity, the account of personal achievement put forward here is preserving in character in regard to the prehistory of personal achievement as a history of preachievements. If the developmental schemes for interactive competence and ego identity are for Habermas, as will be explained later, formal in character and progressive in nature, the preachievements described here are not primarily formal and above all are not developmentally interpreted as inferior, but rather valued for their differences and their enabling character. This preserving, if not conserving, perspective toward the prehistory of personal achievement is intended as a corrective to the solely progressive thrust of Habermas's and other philosophical and social scientific theorizing on individual development. However, my contention is that this "hermeneutics" of life history is also a corrective of a kind that ultimately contributes to the "defense" of subjectivity rather than its demise.

Chapter Overview

The first chapter begins with Gadamer's description of appropriation as an illustration of his more general thesis of the happening structure of understanding. Appropriation is perhaps not as important a concept for Gadamer as many other of the famous concepts in his philosophical hermeneutics that help establish the importance of our situatedness in history. He describes understanding and interpretation as events that "happen" in a manner similar to what happens to a player caught up in the action of a game or a speaker enmeshed in a conversation. Thus the phenomenological descriptions of play and conversation make manifest the happening structure that is also common to understanding, interpretation, and appropriation. Moreover the happening structure of the event also influences Gadamer's conception of *wirkungsgeschichtliches Bewusstsein* as a consciousness of being situated in and being part of an unfinished historical event and, as seen in the discussion of the "truth" of Greek tragedy, as a recognition of human finitude. Therefore the happening structure of the event and the consciousness of *Wirkungsgeschichte* express the importance of our belongingness in history, and they also determine how appropriation is to be understood as event in *Truth and Method*.

These conceptions also influence Paul Ricoeur in his treatment of appropriation in an essay of the same title, so much so that his discussion of appropriation can be considered no more than a preliminary step toward an alternative conception of appropriation that could include both happening and personal accomplishment. In his case as well as Gadamer's, the happening structure of appropriation (1) overshadows the theme of personal achievement through the emphasis placed upon our belongingness to history and tradition, (2) is expressed in the language of event alone or of event "more than" action, and (3) supports and is supported by the consciousness of effective history as a consciousness of limitation.

The second chapter takes up the aspect of the debate between Hans-Georg Gadamer and Jürgen Habermas that is of greatest relevance to the topic of personal achievement; namely, the conflict between *wirkungsgeschichtliches Bewusstsein* and Habermasian self-reflection. These rival conceptions are examined by being situated in the earlier contexts of Gadamer's discussion in *Truth and Method* of *Bildung*, often quite properly translated as "culture," and of Habermas's discussion in *Knowledge and Human Interests* of *Bildungsprozess*, quite properly translated as "self-formative process." It is argued that Gadamer successfully describes a positive sense of belongingness to history, although he also unfortunately seeks to subsume the developmental process of education solely in a belongingness relation to culture. It is further argued that Habermas successfully describes the formative process of *Bildung* as an achievement, but he also overstates what the achievement accomplishes. In *Knowledge and Human Interests*, the interest in emancipation is grounded in the power of self-reflection to dissolve pseudo-natural constraints and to achieve full transparency in its self-genesis. The debate with Gadamer makes evident how these powers, which have their origin in the idealist thinking of Fichte and Hegel, have to be limited by a hermeneutical awareness of historical situatedness.

A careful examination of Gadamer's thesis of historical situatedness, attempted in the following chapter, seeks to distinguish between objections against the conception of self-reflection in *Knowledge and Human Interests* and against the broader aspects of personal achievement. My contention is that Gadamer's objections against the alleged transparency of self-reflection do not disallow a hermeneutical inquiry of a quite different kind into the subject of personal achievement. This kind of hermeneutical inquiry does not emphasize, in the first instance, how historical situatedness limits personal achievment, but rather how it enables achievement or makes it possible. The fundamental complementarity between historical belongingness and personal achievement is conveyed by introducing Habermas's concept of a dynamic "balance" between personal and social identity and modifying it into a balance between the event of historical tradition, understood in much the same way as Gadamer, and the personal act of appropriating that tradition. The basis for this balance is seen to lie in the complementarity between the experiences of belonging to and having achieved within the historical event of tradition.

The attempt to express the proper complementarity between achievement and belongingness must also take into account more recent developments in Habermas's thought. In an impressive accomplishment of self-criticism, he has moved away from the philosophy of reflection to formulate a theory of communication. Within this theory, the process of the appropriation of the self is now located in a theory of the development of ego identity. According to this theory, the ego arises from the interaction of three competences—cognitive, linguistic, and interactive—that develop in a pattern of interaction with three stages: preconventional behavior, conventional behavior, and postconventional behavior. The question remains, however, whether this theory of ego identity may still understate the importance of hermeneutical situatedness.

In the fourth chapter of this study, I argue that this is indeed the case by appealing to a more hermeneutically informed and situated account of ego identity that I find in Erik Erikson. In Erikson's account, the attainment of ego identity is situated as one particular stage in an eight-stage model of the life cycle. It is only one stage of four stages that all fall under Habermas's category of postconventional behavior. More importantly, these stages are not demarcated in terms of competences that are conceived formalistically—that is, in terms of the development of the ability to perform new formal operations at higher-level stages of development. Instead there is an emphasis upon the resolution of more content-oriented conflicts between identity and identity diffusion, intimacy and loneliness, generativity and self-absorption, and ego integrity and despair. The specific conflict involved in the attainment of ego identity displays both the need for personal initiative and the value of fidelity to tradition in the formation of a viable personal identity. This account of ego identity is judged to be an expression of the complementarity between belongingness and achievement superior to the one found in Habermas, at least at this particular stage of his thought with its emphasis upon hypothetical, universalistic reasoning.

In the fifth chapter the reasons why Erikson's theoretical work on ego identity and self-formation is nonetheless hermeneutically situated and grounded are more extensively examined from the point of view of philosophical hermeneutics. The main reason for the hermeneutical situatedness of his theorizing is seen to derive from the fact that he concentrates much of his attention upon some of the same phenomena that have such a central role in Gadamer's *Truth and Method*: play and the process of *Bildung* or self-formation. However, Erikson differs from Gadamer insofar as his descriptions of these processes allow for a much greater role to be ascribed to personal achievement.

Erikson's description of childhood play in *Toys and Reasons* is compared with Gadamer's description of play as already discussed here in chapter 1. Gadamer's description of play discloses it to have a happening structure such that the to-and-fro movement of the game catches its participants up into the event of the play. By contrast, Erikson observes in the protected play of children a desire for—and sense of—individual mastery. This sense of mastery extends to the physical environment and above all to the social experience of the child that is dealt with in play by meditating, experimenting, planning, and sharing. Such mastery is, of course, in even greater evidence in Erikson's descriptions of the "social play" of adolescents in their transition to adulthood. This conception of social play correlates with Gadamer's description of *Bildung*, but it evidences not so much a happening structure as an "action structure" to be characteristic of the process. This action structure—again intended as a complement, not rival, to Gadamer's happening structure—differs from it insofar as it (1) emphasizes, in the first instance, personal achievement rather than belongingness to history and tradition; (2) is expressed in the language of act or accomplishment rather than in the language of event; and, as will be explained in the following chapter, (3) supports and is supported by the consciousness of being able to act or be competent as a consciousness of having been enabled.

In the sixth and final chapter of this study, the process of appropriation is returned to, only now from the point of view of the appropriation of individual life history and the role that consciousness can play in the carrying out of such personal appropriation. The attempt to develop the conception of personal appropriation, together with the description of its accompanying form of consciousness, is made with the aid of an essay by Erikson, "Reflections on Dr. Borg's Life Cycle," on the Ingmar Bergman film *Wild Strawberries*. My interest in the essay lies not in the explicit use Erikson makes of the events of the film as an illustration of his theory of the life cycle. Rather it is in what allows Dr. Borg, the film's central character, to achieve ultimately, according to Erikson, a historical perspective toward his life. This interest is supplemented by my own interpretation of, above all, the final scenes of the film, and both sources are employed in order to introduce a conception of the "consciousness of having been enabled" as playing the crucial role in Borg's personal appropriation of his life history. This consciousness of having been enabled is then compared with Gadamer's conception of *wirkungsgeschichtliches Bewusstsein* and with Habermas's description of the act of self-reflection.

Chapters 5 and 6 concern the differences between, on the one hand, Gadamer and Erikson in relation to the event structure and the action structure of play, and, on the other, Gadamer's conception of the consciousness of having been historically effected and my analysis of the consciousness of having been enabled. The Conclusion takes up a similarity between Erikson and Gadamer that is, in my judgment, of greater import than these differences. This similarity does not concern contents of their thinking but a relationship that is expressed in the "having been" of both consciousnesses. Erikson develops a "preachievement" aspect to his consideration of the topic of personal achievement that parallels the Gadamerian relationship between prejudice and judgment. This preachievement aspect concerns the playfulness of childhood play, which Erikson suggests should remain at the core of all later adolescent and adult activities. This playfulness is to be preserved within individual life history in the same manner that tradition and historical belongingness are preserved in history according to Gadamer.

With the observance of this similarity, the contours take final shape of an approach to life history that acknowledges it as an important subject in its own right and yet does not deny the importance of historical situatedness. Such an approach does not play the themes of historical belongingness and personal achievement off one another, but rather allows the description of play to have prominent and equal aspects of both features in the structures of its event and action. Such an approach does not argue against the consciousness of having been historically effected, but does argue for the consciousness of having been enabled as having an equally prominent role in the formulation and completion of individual life history.

Finally, such an approach explicates and emphasizes the importance of preservation—in both history and life history, of both historical connectedness and childhood playfulness, and through consciousness of both historical prejudgment and personal preachievement. These are the contours of an approach that, according to my understanding, merits the nomenclature of a philosophical hermeneutical treatment of the subject of life history, even if certain traditional polemical comparisons on the limits of personal achievement are noteworthy only in their absence.

1

The Event of Appropriation in Philosophical Hermeneutics

Appropriation has not been the most central theme for the thinkers most identified with philosophical hermeneutics. The concept of *Aneignung*, translated in the original English edition by either "appropriation" or "assimilation" depending upon the context, appears often in Hans-Georg Gadamer's *Truth and Method*; appropriation is made the explicit title of an important hermeneutical essay by Paul Ricoeur. Nevertheless when the theme of appropriation is taken up by either Gadamer or Ricoeur, it is given a less prominent role than in works by earlier hermeneutical authors. If, for example, appropriation is considered in Ricoeur's essay as perhaps the first theme of Romantic hermeneutics, for Ricoeur himself it is the last major theme. For Gadamer the same is true, if appropriation can be considered a major theme at all.

Consequently this chapter begins not by directly exploring Gadamer's conception of appropriation, but rather by examining other of his more famous and important concepts. All these concepts direct attention toward the reality, and support the importance, of our belongingness to history. One of the most central concepts is, of course, understanding, which is conceived as an event that happens to one and catches one up, similar to what happens to a player in a game or a speaker in a conversation. Gadamer's phenomenological descriptions of play and conversation display a happening structure that is common to play and conversation, and to understanding and appropriation as well. This happening structure is elucidated and employed in turn to situate consciousness within the event of play, of conversation, and ultimately of tradition and history. Consequently, another of the most central concepts, *wirkungsgeschichtliches Bewusstsein* or "historically effected consciousness," involves a consciousness of belonging to a Gadamerian fusion of horizons and an awareness of the limitations of subjectivity. Especially the treatment of truth as the disclosure of human finitude in Gadamer's discussion of tragedy makes it clear how *wirkungsgeschichtliches Bewusstsein* involves both the consciousness of human finitude and the finitude of human consciousness. Therefore any exploration of Gadamer's conception of appropriation must consider first at least two of his more central conceptions: the happening structure of play, conversation, and the event of understanding, and the consciousness of *Wirkungsgeschichte* as an awareness of both belongingness and limitation. Both of these conceptions establish for Gadamer the fact that appropriation is a happening or event of history more than it is our action upon what is appropriated.

The next section of this chapter will take up Paul Ricoeur's conception of appropriation as it is explicitly developed in the essay of the same title. Ricoeur's conception of appropriation will be introduced by way of his distinction between participatory belongingness and distanciation, and its contrast to Gadamer's sole emphasis upon belongingness. However, it will also be seen to be bound by the same major concerns as are expressed in Gadamer's hermeneutics. Thus while Ricoeur calls appropriation a major, but final, theme of his hermeneutics, it is similarly both elucidated and affected by Gadamer's phenomenological description of play as a happening and the accompanying emphasis upon human limitation. Hence his conception occupies the position of an intermediate step on the way toward an alternative conception of appropriation that might truly incorporate a different aspect of accomplishment and achievement.

The final section will return to the subject of the happening structure of play, conversation, and understanding. It will focus on the relationship of the individual to the carrying out of the event and argue that the human role of carrying out the event of understanding overshadows and indeed displaces the perspective of human "subject." Gadamer's criticisms of subjectivity are surveyed in this context and the full implications of the happening structure of play are enumerated and assayed. This description of the "event structure" of play will serve as the basis of comparison for the description of an "action structure" of play to be attempted in a later chapter.

The Happening Structure of Understanding and Effective History

The consideration of the topic of appropriation from the point of view of philosophical hermeneutics can begin with the shift in meaning of the term that occurs in Martin Heidegger's later philosophy. This shift in meaning involves the happening nature of the disclosure of Being in his later thought. Translators of the later writings of Heidegger usually decide to translate *das Ereignis* not as "the event" or "the happening" or "the occurrence," but as "appropriation" or "the disclosure of appropriation." Part of the reason that one translator has made this decision is explained as follows:

> It is clear that Heidegger here is making use of the "own" meaning of *"eigen"* to read the sense of the verb *ereignen* as *to make one's own, to appropriate.* But instead of "appropriate" in the sense of one's own appropriating of something for oneself, for which the verb *sich (etwas) aneignen* is already available, Heidegger wants to speak of an activity or process by which nothing "selfish" occurs, but rather by which the different members of the world are brought into belonging to and with one another and are helped to realize themselves and each other in realizing this belonging.[1]

Although Gadamer does not adopt the vocabulary of *Ereignis* but chooses his own term, *Geschehen*, it will be shown in this section how this very central concept[2] has been influenced by the same shift in emphasis. In particular, attention will be directed to how much Gadamer's own concept of event or happening may be understood and broadly interpreted as a "disclosure of appropriation" and to what extent this concept governs the way he comprehends the concept of appropriation (*Aneignung*) more narrowly understood.

The first important reference to *Geschehen* occurs in Part One of *Truth and Method*, entitled "The question of truth as it emerges in the experiences of art." There Gadamer writes that "all encounter with the language of art is an encounter with a still unfinished event (*einem unabgeschlossenen Geschehen*) and is itself part of the event" (T&M, 88). As Joel Weinsheimer observes in his commentary to *Truth and Method*, the sentence actually "beggars translation" (GH, 99). The past participle *unabgeschlossen* means, among other things, "unlocked, unclosed, open, disclosed, unconcluded, inconclusive, inclusive" and its connotations are "negative, double negative, and positive" (GH,

100). In this way a process is described that has both continuity and change but without closure. However, it is in the second part of Gadamer's statement—that all encounter is itself part of the event—that an even more crucial element for understanding the nature of the process is given, for it is this part that states that the encounter itself is included in both the continuity and the change, and offers no prospect for closure of its own.

This feature of the inclusiveness of the encounter in the *Geschehen* is elucidated in reference to the work of art through Gadamer's phenomenological description of play. Gadamer writes that play is the way of being of the work of art: "When we speak of play in the context of the experience of art, play does not mean the behavior or even the disposition of the creators or the enjoyers of art, and not at all the freedom of a subjectivity that dabbles in play, but rather the way of being of the artwork itself" (T&M, 91). For Gadamer the player of the game is someone who brings forth the way in which the game is: "The subject of the game is not the player; rather the players are merely the way the play comes into presentation" (T&M, 92). And the spectators to whom the play is presented are similarly not outside the play of the game but caught up within its presentation.

Consequently the subject of Gadamer's phenomenological description of play is the play itself. However, this is not to be taken as a literal truth. The important thing that it says is that the play is not an object; it is not an activity that a subject consciously engages in. Instead "all playing is a being played" (T&M, 95), which again is not intended to make the reverse implication that the player is the object of the game. Rather what is meant is that play is an event that happens to its players or even "plays" them as Jean Grondin explains in his book, *Hermeneutische Wahrheit? Zum Wahrheitsbegriff Hans-Georg Gadamers*:

> However the state of being taken in (*das Eingenommensein*) does not arise from us, but characterizes the peculiar activity (*das eigentümliche Tun*) of the game itself. ... The concept of play above all takes into account *phenomenologically* the being caught up (*Ergriffenwerden*) by the happening of truth. According to the *form* a new category is therefore found out that makes possible the overcoming of subjectivity and points to a new "subject" of truth. This new subject appears as a reality exceeding us, to whose share a superiority according to *content* consequently falls over and against ourselves. [HW, 104–5]

The same inclusiveness or ability of the event character or happening structure to "take in" its participants resurfaces in another very important phenomenological description in Part Three of *Truth and Method*. Gadamer's formulation employed in the analysis of the work of art refers to an encounter with the language of art. In Part Three, the clarification is given that language is to be understood as the medium of disclosure of our experience of the world, and not as an objectification of the world. Moreover conversation is designated as the point of departure for an ontology of human understanding. In this role conversation is conceived as mediating the disclosure of language. It, like play, has the character of an event exceeding us—as its description makes clear.

What concerns Gadamer in his description of conversation is not what either of the speaking partners individually brings to the conversation in mediating between one another. Instead it is what is common to them or, more exactly, what language makes common to them in disclosing the world. The subject matter or *Sache* of the conversation can seize the conversationalists and take them up in an event with a happening character. The attainment of mediation is often unguided and even unwilled by the individuals concerned, as Gadamer explains:

> Thus a fundamental conversation is never one that we intend to conduct. Rather, it is generally more correct to say we fall into a conversation, or even that we become entangled in it. The way in which one word follows another, with the conversation taking its own turnings and reaching its own conclusion, may well be conducted in some way, but the people conversing are far less the leaders of it than the led. ... Understanding or its failure is like an event (*Geschehen*) which is performed (*vollzogen*) upon us. [T&M, 345; translation of final sentence modified by me]

Again it turns out that the speakers of the conversation are not its subjects, nor is the matter of the discussion its object. There is no distinct subject or object at all, but an event of understanding that is brought about by the "play" of the conversation.

If language is an event, it certainly also parallels Gadamer's discussion of event in art insofar as it is *unabgeschlossen* as well. The event of language is an event of handing over or *Überlieferung*, a word that is translated both as tradition and as transmission, but in any case conveys a carrying over into the present:

> Language constitutes the hermeneutical event proper not
> as language, whether as grammar or as lexicon, but in the
> coming into language of that which has been said in tradi-
> tion (*Überlieferung*), an event that is at once appropriation
> and interpretation. Thus here it really is true to say that
> this event is not our action upon the thing [*Sache*: issue,
> subject matter], but the act of the thing itself. [T&M, 421]

As is stated clearly, understanding is not an action of subjectivity, but
rather "a standing within a happening of tradition [or an occurrence
of transmission: *Überlieferungsgeschehen*]" (T&M, 258). Tradition
happens in a way that can be said to be a working out of itself. Weinsheimer provides a useful and thorough discussion of a set of terms
that cluster around the working out of history:

> *Wirkung* is related to *wirken* (knit, weave, integrate), to
> *verwirklichen* (realize, make real), and to *Wirklichkeit* (reality,
> actuality). *Wirkungsgeschichte* is the reality of history in that
> it is the history of realization. What is real works—that is,
> in realizing itself it works itself out. . . . Wirkung, then,
> means work in the transitive sense. History is Wirkungsge-
> schichte in that it works something or works on something:
> it effects and has an effect. The effect of history—its reali-
> zation, its reality—is history. [GH, 181]

The event by which tradition "comes into language" is "an event of
transmission (*Überlieferungsgeschehen*) in which past and present are
constantly being mediated" (T&M, 258).

The mediation between past and present is expressed through
another one of Gadamer's central concepts, the fusing or melding of
horizons (*Horizontverschmelzung*). This concept contains metaphors that
again suggest that transmission is accomplished by an act of the thing,
and not by our action upon the thing. As the thing works itself out, as
it is transmitted into the present, it changes, but the change is to be
attributed to the *Wirkung* of the thing into the present. Every present
understanding is a different understanding, but this fact does not
imply a gulf between past and present. Instead there is a continual
transmission of tradition that is expressed by the fusing of horizons:

> The horizon of the present does not take shape at all
> without the past. There is just as little a horizon of the
> present in itself as there are historical horizons which one
> would have to attain. Rather, understanding is always the
> procedure of the fusion of such horizons allegedly existing
> in themselves. [T&M, 273]

Modern historical research does not occur outside the fusion of horizons: "Modern historical research itself is not only research, but the transmission of tradition" (T&M, 253). Of course the great temporal distance (*Zeitabstand*) between the present and some past historical horizons can make the researcher aware of how different the understanding of his research subject has become. In other words, the researcher can become conscious of *Wirkungsgeschichte*, the way that the past has worked itself out through a long process into the present. But this *wirkungsgeschichtliches Bewusstsein*, or consciousness of effective history, does not involve the assumption of a position outside the past. The understanding it brings is itself "essentially, an effective-historical process" (T&M, 267).

Gadamer asserts that a proper hermeneutics "would have to demonstrate the effectiveness of history within understanding itself" (T&M, 267). This comment recalls his earlier comment about art that the encounter with the language of art is itself "part of" the *unabgeschlossenes Geschehen*. The consciousness of effective history is for Gadamer in a quite profound sense a consciousness of being a part of the event, of being a part of history. The players of the game, the conversation partners, and the historical researcher are all part of the event that catches them up. Of course we are as well, as Grondin explains: "Understanding stands under an effect which can never become transparent to it. Only *subsequently* do we ascertain that we have 'understood'" (HW, 127). We belong to history and the consciousness of effective history should manifest to us our belongingness.

Gadamer is very explicit about this important result of our consciousness of effective history: "In truth history does not belong to us, but we belong to it" (T&M, 245). It is because of this belongingness of understanding to history itself that Gadamer claims that *wirkungsgeschichtliches Bewusstsein* is more being than awareness.

Weinsheimer explains why belongingness is in reference to the being level of effective historical consciousness more than the level of consciousness:

> The dialectical changes that occur in the process of inter-
> pretation are not a function of the interpreter's subjectivity
> but of tradition. . . . History is made in the event of under-
> standing tradition, but this history is not a mere passage of
> time, for in interpretation tradition comes into being.
> There is an access of being in the same way as when, in a
> genuine conversation, something occurs to both partners
> that had not occurred to either of them before. When they

come to an understanding, something new is conceived.
Something new happens, and what occurs in hermeneutic
conversation is being.

We come to realize that belonging is an ontological way
of talking about the condition achieved by the fusion of
horizons. [GH, 250–51]

While Weinsheimer provides an insightful analysis of the relation of belongingness to interpretation, another aspect of belongingness needs to be explored. In part of a quotation from Gadamer that
was not discussed earlier, it is remarked that the event of language is
both appropriation and interpretation. Moreover, one of his most
important hermeneutical theses is that all interpretation is at the
same time application. What about the relationship of belongingness
to the major theme of this chapter, appropriation? Despite the fact
that the word *Aneignung* is used by Gadamer, which could connote a
more subjective process of appropriation, is it also the case with it,
like interpretation, that the changes that occur are to be accorded to
the working out of the *Geschehen* of tradition and not the appropri-
ator's subjectivity? Again, in Weinsheimer's terms, is it the event of
tradition, and tradition alone, that comes into being in
appropriation?

To answer these questions, it is necessary to explicate further
the theme of truth in *Truth and Method*. The discussion of truth that is
most relevant to the theme of appropriation occurs in the context of
Gadamer's analysis of the work of art.[3] It concerns Greek tragedy and
entails for us a filling out of the transition that is made from the
phenomenological description of "play" to the analysis of "a play." A
play has a *Gebilde* or structure for Gadamer, but it may be more accurate to say that the play is the *Gebilde* or even that the *Gebilde* is the
play. The *Gebilde* of the play is repeatable in its performances, but the
play must not be viewed as something outside its performance.
Instead the play exists in its performance and, as its performance is
repeated, its way of being differs even as it remains itself: "The task
of the performance is to mediate the work in such a way that the
medium is not differentiated from what is mediated. The past must
be *made* manifest to the present because its presence and immediacy
are not given" (GH, 115). In this comment it can be seen that the
performance of the play functions like interpretation with respect to
history: both are ways that the play or tradition respectively happen.

But the play, or more specifically the Greek tragedy, also has
an effect upon the spectator. This effect or *Wirkung* is related to what
Aristotle writes about the catharsis of tragedy. Gadamer explains:

"Being overcome by misery and terror presents a painful schism. In it there is a disunion with what is happening, a not wanting it to be true, a refusal to acknowledge the horrible event. Just this however is the effect (*Wirkung*) of the tragic catastrophe, that the schism from what is, is dissolved" (T&M, 116). The dissolution of the schism is achieved by the acceptance of the spectator, an acceptance and perhaps even an affirmation of the truth of the play. But what is the truth that the tragedy discloses? Again Weinsheimer provides a useful commentary:

> The great ones of the earth are, like us, caught up in events that are larger than they, events that expose the littleness of knowing, feeling, doing—the littleness of subjectivity—in the face of the frightful immensity of what happens. In tragedy the insistence of history on and in consciousness is dramatized. The truth of tragedy, the game that is played with us, protagonist and spectator alike, cannot be proved, still less evaded, but only admitted. For the truth is something that we can do nothing about. [GH, 116–17]

The truth—that we are finite creatures—is indeed something that we can do nothing about. But the reference back to the phenomenological description of the game ("the game is played with us") suggests that the appropriation of the truth is also something that we do not do either. As Gadamer writes of the spectator: "It is the truth of his own world, the religious and moral world in which he lives, *that presents itself to him* and in which he represents himself" (T&M, 113; italics added).

Nor is the situation fundamentally different for the playwright. Gadamer writes, "The free invention of the poet is the presentation of a common truth that is binding on the poet as well" (T&M, 118). It appears, then, that this common truth is working its own self out, that it is the origin of its own effective history, that it is the something new disclosed in the work of art that the artist must bring forth and the spectator must appropriate. In this respect the appeal to the way of being of the work of art accomplishes much the same for Gadamer as it did for Heidegger in his essay on the origin of the work of art. For Heidegger the creator of the work of art is not a free and innovative genius, but rather someone who brings forth the workly nature of the work; similarly the preserver of the work of art is someone who lets the truth of the work of art be. For both Heidegger and Gadamer, the way of being of the work of art as a "disclosure of appropriation" delineates the way that the truth of the work of art is appropriated by both the artist and the spectator. The *Ereignis* or *Geschehen* structure respectively governs how the process of appropriation (*Aneignung*) is understood.

Ricoeur on Appropriation

Paul Ricoeur's conception of philosophical hermeneutics clearly distinguishes itself from Gadamer's, but represents at best an intermediate step with respect to a more prominent and more active construal of personal appropriation. In contrast to Gadamer's "consciousness of belonging which is expressly defined by the rejection of distanciation" (H&HS, 61), Ricoeur advocates a historical consciousness that "seeks not simply to repudiate distanciation but assume it" (H&HS, 61). However, his views on the theme of appropriation subordinate this theme to the larger event of disclosure in a manner that recalls very much both Gadamer and Heidegger. Therefore many of the main themes of Ricoeur's conception of philosophical hermeneutics will be elucidated, but primarily in the role of a transitional step to a fundamentally different conception of personal appropriation as both happening and accomplishment.

The interrelationship between participatory belonging and distanciation is developed by Ricoeur in the context of his distinction between writing and speaking.[4] This distinction in turn relates to another very important distinction between meaning and event. There is both a fleeting historical event or "saying" and an enduring meaning or "said" in every act of written or spoken communication. The role of meaning, however, is especially evident in writing, for the meaning is inscribed in symbols that are detachable from their immediate circumstances. Because of this "distancing" of writing from its context, it is accorded a "semantic autonomy" that allows it to be treated as an ideal entity and not simply as "the expression of certain socio-cultural needs and as a response to certain perplexities well localized in space and time" (IT, 90). As an ideal entity that is decontextualized from its historical circumstances, the written text is subject to methodological forms of inquiry. However, Ricoeur differs from Gadamer in deeming methods of structural explanation and methodical hermeneutical interpretation as productive and not alienating: "Productive distance means methodological distanciation" (IT, 89). Therefore participatory belonging and distanciation are both necessary and both positive features of the ontological relationship of historical consciousness to history.

Distanciation is contrasted by Ricoeur not only to participatory belonging, but also to appropriation as well. In his essay "Appropriation" he writes, "Appropriation is thus a dialectical concept: the counterpart of the timeless distanciation implied by any literary or textual criticism of an anti-historicist character" (H&HS, 185). In this contrast, the comparison is between the timeless inscription or objectification of meaning that is "a necessary mediation between the writer and reader" (H&HS, 185) and "a complementary act of a more existential character" (H&HS, 185) that is the appropriation of meaning. This term is a translation for *Aneignung* in German, but it is not related so much to a subjective act of making one's own as rather to the general hermeneutical goal of struggling against cultural distance and historical alienation. What I am to appropriate is a proposed world, "not *behind* the text as a hidden intention would be, but *in front of* it, as that which *the work* unfolds, discovers, reveals" (H&HS, 143; final italics are added).

Ricoeur explicitly refers to Gadamer's description and analysis of play in developing his own conception of appropriation. This description and analysis are of course quite familiar. It comes as no surprise, therefore, when Ricoeur characterizes what he terms as the more "existential" act of appropriation in terms of a "letting go": "Appropriation is also *and primarily* a 'letting go' " (H&HS, 191; italics added). The ego that appropriates the text must relinquish itself to the text in the same way that players abandon themselves in becoming caught up in the play of the game. In fact Ricoeur states explicitly that "understanding is as much disappropriation as appropriation" (H&HS, 144). Thus for Ricoeur appropriation is indeed an important theme in philosophical hermeneutics and it clearly has a personal or existential aspect, but it is the last theme subordinated to more important themes such as revelation or disclosure: "appropriation is the process by which the revelation of new modes of being . . . *gives* the subject new capacities for knowing himself" (H&HS, 192). Therefore the "enlarged self" of the subject who allows itself to be caught up by the world "in front of" the text is received, not achieved (H&HS, 143).

Ricoeur's almost paradoxical statement that understanding involves as much disappropriation as appropriation or, in another turn of phrase, that appropriation is dispossession as much as possession, has a laudatory function in the context of earlier Romantic conceptions of philosophical hermeneutics and their underlying philosophy of subjectivity. These conceptions make appropriation the first theme of philosophical hermeneutics and interpret the text as an objective projection of the author who possesses the key to the interpretive process. But if the Romantic conception of appropriation is exaggerated and ultimately incorrect, Ricoeur's characterization of the personal process of appropriation may at least be suspected of going too far in the opposite respect. The appeal to disappropriation, dispossession, and relinquishment serves to limit the excessive claims of subjectivity, but this appeal also ensures that the personal act of appropriation is understood in terms of event and event alone. In this respect Ricoeur is in full agreement with Gadamer, as the comparison of both their views shows.

Weinsheimer gives a perhaps clearer account of the implications of Gadamer's analysis of play for the subject than is present in *Truth and Method* itself:

> Dance is the dancing of it, the game itself is the playing of
> it, and the artwork itself exists only in its working, only in
> its being experienced. The experience of art is not experi-
> ence by a subject, for the subject is not itself. It is altered
> in experience. And it is not experience of an object,
> because the subject is altered, has an experience, only if it
> does not objectify the artwork. [GH, 103]

If the interpretation of Ricoeur on the theme of appropriation is correct, he concurs with everything in this analysis except for the final implication that objectified experience or methodological distanciation cannot be productive for the subject. On the other themes he writes, for example, in *Hermeneutics and the Human Sciences*: "A work opens up its readers and thus creates its own subjective *vis-a-vis*" (H&HS, 143). And in *The Conflict of Interpretations*, he states even more decisively of the subject: "He is a being who discovers, by the exegesis of his own life, that he is placed in being before he places and possesses himself. In this way, hermeneutics would discover a manner of existing which would remain from start to finish a *being-interpreted*" (CI, 11). Hence for Ricoeur as for Gadamer, as the play of the game is more a being played than a playing on the part of the subject, so the being a part of the larger event of appropriation is a being interpreted rather than an interpreting.

The closeness of Ricoeur to Gadamer on the theme of appropriation can be illustrated in a final and conclusive way through a phrase that originates with Ricoeur and is taken up in Weinsheimer's commentary on Gadamer. In *Freud and Philosophy: An Essay on Interpretation*, Ricoeur writes of the interpreter who understands the text with an attitude of faith in terms of a second naïveté:

The contrary of suspicion, I will say bluntly, is faith. What faith? No longer, to be sure, the first faith of the simple soul, but rather the second faith of one who has engaged in hermeneutics, faith that has undergone criticism, post-critical faith. . . . It is a rational faith, for it interprets, but it is a faith because it seeks, through interpretation, a second naiveté. [SF, 28]

In a similar manner, Weinsheimer writes in regard to Gadamer:

All the effort that goes into building the hermeneutic consciousness of language is directed toward making the interpreter's words and concepts just as transparent and invisible as they are in naive interpretation. Understanding reaches its highest sophistication in this second naiveté— when it recedes, effaces itself and simply lets the text speak through it without interference. [GH, 225–26]

The Happening Structure of Appropriation

Weinsheimer's description of the second naivety of under-standing recalls a similar quotation from Gadamer himself on the process of interpretation: "All genuine interpretation of linguistic texts, not just grammatical interpretation, seems to me to disappear in this way. Interpretation must play, that is, it must come into play, in order to negate itself in its own achievement" (PH, 127). According to the first section of this chapter, the reference to play is not fortui-tous, but the explanatory key for understanding how the act of inter-pretation is included in the event of the *Überlieferung* of the text. It is the *Geschehen* structure of play that governs how interpretation and understanding are understood—and not just for Gadamer but for Ricoeur as well.

However, the reference to play in Gadamer's quotation is not important only for the way that it includes interpretation in the working out of the text. Gadamer claims that interpretation must come into play in order to disappear and to "negate itself in its own achievement." This claim recalls the earlier comment from the trans-lator of Heidegger that the disclosure of appropriation is conceived in such a way that nothing "selfish" occurs, that the sense of one's own appropriating of something for oneself is not intended. More specifically to this point, Otto Pöggeler has commented in an essay on

Heidegger concerning the event or *Ereignis* structure of the way of being of the work of art, the thing, and language: "Man is no longer thought of as a 'subject', but rather as the one who has to carry out the event of appropriation."[5] If the parallel between Gadamer and Heidegger is so close in this regard for both the work of art and language, then it must also be inquired whether Pöggeler's comment does not also pertain to Gadamer and his views about the role of human beings in the working out of history.

The applicability of Pöggeler's comment to Gadamer appears to be admitted in the earlier quotation from Grondin, which spoke of the "overcoming of subjectivity" and the new "subject" of truth as a "reality exceeding us." It appears to be secured even further when Gadamer's criticisms of subjectivity are also brought to bear. These criticisms of the subject are supported by his views on interpretation and appropriation, which indeed are at the heart of his general conception of philosophical hermeneutics. This conception depends heavily on the persistence of the event character of history and on the limitations of the consciousness that becomes aware of history. These complementary hermeneutical theses about our belongingness to history are used to establish the situatedness of consciousness in the very events that are sought to be understood and appropriated. The fact that we belong to history means:

> *All* understanding is self understanding, but not in the
> sense of a preliminary self-possession or of one finally and
> definitively achieved. For the self-understanding only real-
> izes itself in the understanding of a subject matter and
> does not have the character of a free self-realization. The
> self we are does not possess itself; one could say that it
> "happens." [PH, 55]

We are not independent over and against history, and to become conscious of this fact is to become conscious of the way tradition works itself "beyond our willing and doing" (W&M, xvi) and to recognize the deep ontological continuity of the fusion of horizons. Gadamer even goes on to say, as was noted earlier in the Introduction, that "the self-awareness of the individual is only a flickering in the closed circuit of historical life" (T&M, 245).

The thesis that consciousness is always situated in the event or happening of tradition and history is a crucial claim from Gadamer that must also be a central part in any hermeneutical philosophy. It issues from equally important theses concerning the event character of language and history, and the self-limiting character of the consciousness that becomes aware of history. Indeed it is the happening structure of the event, established by Gadamer's description of play, that has the most pivotal role, for it is this structure that describes how the consciousness of being historically effected is indeed "part of the event," "caught up" in it, "taken in." Thus it is this structure that discloses the belongingness to history, which is so essential to philosophical hermeneutics that it is what consciousness becomes conscious of, and is so favorably contrasted to human willing and doing and individual self-awareness. The process of appropriation (*Aneignung*) is described the way it is by Gadamer and Ricoeur, because it exemplifies this happening structure of play with all its attendant implications concerning historical belongingness.

Gadamer's description of the event character of history and tradition conveys a central insight from Heidegger, which must be given its due. Nevertheless it will be questioned later whether belongingness to history has to be conceived solely in Gadamer's manner and subjectivity so severely criticized in order to establish the thesis that consciousness is situated. Do interpretation and appropriation always have to be considered in terms of event and event alone? Does appropriation have other aspects besides the working out of history as the role for human beings? Would these aspects allow the human subject to play a more active role in the process? Does the viewpoint toward human beings as subjects always have to distort or at least mislead in the carrying out of the event of appropriation?

These are questions that will not be answered here but will be resituated into another description of human play and the work of art of a five-year-old in chapter 5. A different description of the phenomenon of play will be advanced at that time, one that focuses on the desire and sense for individual mastery. This description will be seen to involve a different structure than Gadamer's event structure, an action structure that will be compared in its basic features with the emphasis upon historical belongingness over personal achievement and the self-limiting character of consciousness that have been described above. The aim will not be to overturn or supplant this very important characterization of play, but rather to complement it with another description that is equally fundamental to the phenomenon.

Before this comparison is attempted, the central theses of Gadamer concerning the persistence of the event character of tradition and the hermeneutical situatedness of historically effected consciousness need to be examined more closely in order to assess, on the one hand, what they quite justifiably entail and, on the other, where they may be overstated. However, this examination will not take place in regard to the concept of appropriation, but a very closely allied concept, *Bildung*, which is another of the very central concepts of *Truth and Method*. In his discussion of the process of *Bildung*, Gadamer positions himself with respect to Hegel's understanding of the same process and with respect to Hegel's philosophy in general. Moreover he also positions himself with respect to Jürgen Habermas, who is developing his own understanding of *Bildungsprozess*, understood as "process of self-formation," in what can be interpreted as his reinterpretation of Hegelian thought in *Knowledge and Human Interests*. Both Habermas's interpretation of *Bildungsprozess* and Gadamer's interpretation of *Bildung* are important and useful indications of how they conceive of the relationship between historical belongingness and personal achievement in their debate, although of course that was not the immediate concern of either of their interpretations.

The next chapter will present these two interpretations of education and self-formation. The chapter after it will examine more closely the precise implications of Gadamer's thesis of hermeneutical situatedness and the concept of *wirkungsgeschichtliches Bewusstsein* for the possibility and importance of personal achievement.

2

Gadamer and Habermas on the Process of *Bildung*

n many ways the debate between Hans-Georg Gadamer and Jürgen Habermas is an important point of departure and primary source for this study on personal achievement. However, this debate does not play these roles in the way in which it progressively develops into competing claims concerning the universality of the ontology of philosophical hermeneutics and the universality of rationally reconstructive sciences. In fact this is the very sort of opposition that is sought to be avoided. Hence the strategy that is undertaken here is not to assess the debate globally and in its progressive movement, but only partially and, in a particular sense, backwards. Thus only the rival conceptions of historical consciousness and self-reflection are examined, and these are interpreted backwards in the direction of Gadamer's discussion in *Truth and Method* of *Bildung* and of Habermas's discussion in *Knowledge and Human Interests* of *Bildungsprozess*. While these descriptions do play an important role in the one aspect of the debate of our concern, they are otherwise in the background of the dispute. Nevertheless they are of greater relevance to the theme of personal achievement than all the other aspects of the debate. Therefore the treatments of *Bildung* and *Bildungsprozess* will be discussed and evaluated primarily as they appear in the two major works of Gadamer and Habermas, and as they affect the debate, rather than beginning with the primary subject matter of the debate itself.

The quite differing importances that Gadamer and Habermas place upon historical belongingness and personal achievement issue from their opposing understandings of a common vocabulary: for Gadamer, *Bildung*; for Habermas, *Bildungsprozess*. These terms will usually be left untranslated, but an initial understanding of them may be conveyed through a translator's note to *Knowledge and Human Interests*:

> *Bildung* means both formation or shaping and the (human-istic) education, cultivation, and acculturation of a self-conscious subject. *Bildungsprozess* has been translated as "self-formative process" in the sense of a personal or cultural process of growth and development. "Self-forma-tive" does not imply the realization of a plan chosen in advance by the self, but a process in which the self never-theless participates. [K&HI, 320n]

The Hegelian origin of this vocabulary is obvious, although in Gadamer's case crucial meanings of the term *Bildung* antecede Hegel. In addition, his interest, like Hegel's, is in the formation, develop-ment, and education of a people, or the human race, or human beings generically as much as, if not more than, in the *Bildung* of an individual self. Thus, although he and Habermas share a Hegelian background in their discussion of *Bildung*, they disagree in the emphasis they place upon the different features involved in the process. Moreover while they, like virtually all contemporary philoso-phers who have an opinion on the subject, concur in denying the possibility of absolute knowledge and the role it plays in Hegel's description of a processs of self-recognition on the part of absolute spirit, they differ in their interpretation of the consequences that follow from this denial. Hence a comparison of Gadamer and Habermas on the topic of *Bildung* also necessarily involves, at least at this stage in Habermas's thought, a comparison of their differing standpoints toward Hegel, even if this is not the manner in which Habermas, for example, would consider his own work.[1] The purpose of this chapter is to offer such a comparison as a means for eluci-dating their differing estimations of the importance of historical consciousness and the power of self-reflection.

Retracing the *Phenomenology* Backward I

In the Introduction to *Truth and Method*, Gadamer writes:

The conceptual framework in which philosophy develops has always already captivated us in the same way the language we live in determines us. Thus conscientious thought must become conscious of this captivation. A new critical consciousness must now accompany all responsible philosophy and place before the forum of historical tradition to which we all belong the habits of speech and thought which are formed (*bilden*) in the individual's communication with his environment. The following investigation endeavors to fulfill this demand by combining as closely as possible an inquiry into the history of concepts with the substantive exposition of its theme. [T&M, xv]

One of the most important concepts to have "always already" captivated Gadamer's philosophical hermeneutics and that accompanies the substantive exposition of its major themes is *Bildung*. Of *Bildung* Gadamer writes, "The concept of self-formation or cultivation (*Begriff der Bildung*), which became supremely important at the time, was perhaps the greatest idea of the eighteenth century, and precisely this concept indicates the element in which the nineteenth-century *Geisteswissenschaften* lived, even if they did not know how to justify it epistemologically" (T&M, 10).

During the eighteenth century alluded to by Gadamer, the meaning of the word *Bildung* is detached from any association with natural shapes or forms, and becomes intimately associated with the idea of culture. Herder writes of a "rising up" or *Emporbildung* to humanity so that "at this stage Bildung means the specifically human way of coming into one's own (*ausbilden*) through enculturation" (GH, 69). This process is distinguished from, and held to be more than, the process of cultivating talents or habits. The cultivation of a talent "is the development of something that is given, so that the practice and cultivation of it is a mere means to an end" (T&M, 12). *Bildung* differs from cultivation insofar as it is not the development of something latent but rather the acquisition of potency. Moreover the result of acquiring potency cannot be separated from the process by which the potency is acquired. Gadamer writes of this process, in distinction from cultivation:

> Bildung [*sic*], contrariwise, that by which and through which one is formed becomes completely one's own. To some extent everything that is received is absorbed, but in Bildung what is absorbed is not like a means that has lost its function. Rather in acquired Bildung nothing disappears, but everything is preserved. Bildung is a genuine

historical idea, and precisely this historical character of "preservation" is at stake for the understanding of the *Geisteswissenschaften*. [T&M, 12; translation of final sentence modified by me]

Gadamer follows Hegel in the further explication of the concept of *Bildung*. *Bildung* involves for Hegel progress away from immediacy and particularity toward universality. Work plays a prominent role in this progress insofar as making things rather than consuming them requires the restraining of immediate desires and of particular needs for the sake of later gratification. When "a man gives himself over to his work so wholly that it becomes distanced from his personal needs and private desires, he not only allows what he makes to assume its own form but does the same to himself" (GH, 69); or, in Hegel's words, "by forming the thing, it [the subject] forms itself" (T&M, 13). The progress toward the universal is seen practically in the adoption of a profession that "asks of one to give oneself to tasks that one would not seek out as a private aim" (T&M, 14).

Theoretical *Bildung* also goes beyond what one knows and experiences immediately. Hegel suggests that the world and language of the ancients are especially appropriate for this aspect of self-formation. In Weinsheimer's words, "Understanding this world, given its remoteness from ours, necessitates the self-alienation that is the initial movement of Bildung; yet ancient art, literature, and philosophy also offer the possibility of returning to ourselves with a better self-understanding" (GH, 69–70). Gadamer finds in this sentiment the prejudice of the classical gymnasium director that Hegel was,[2] but also a basically correct insight: "To find one's own in the alien, to become at home in it, is the fundamental movement of spirit, whose being is only return to itself from being otherwise" (T&M, 15). Weinsheimer comments on this passage:

> In this structure of excursion and return we discern the circular structure of hermeneutic understanding. Already we can see why it is not a vicious circle in which the mind just spins its wheels. The spirit consists in movement—first in its departure from its home into the strange and unfamiliar, the otherwise. If the move is complete, the spirit finds a home, makes itself a home in the other, so that its new home is no longer alien. But at this point, the elsewhere that had once seemed so foreign proves to be not only a new home but its real home; we discover that the movement which before had seemed to be an exile was in

fact a homecoming, and what had seemed to be home
when we set out was in fact merely a way station. [GH, 70]

As Grondin writes in another context: "We stand over and against tradition not as something foreign, but as our own, yes, as our ownmost self" (HW, 147).

If the being of spirit for Gadamer is only return, then the self becomes and is only at the end and not at the beginning of *Bildung*. Moreover the return involves the preservation of what is returned from initially as supposedly alien, but what turns out to be a new and real homecoming. Such preservation is not restricted to theoretical *Bildung*, for it is merely a continuation of a fundamental process of *Bildung* that begins much earlier. Gadamer claims that every "single individual that raises himself out of his natural being to the spiritual finds in the language, customs and institutions of his people a pre-given body of material which, as in learning to speak, he has to make his own" (T&M, 15).

To go back to an earlier quotation, the individual is "always already" caught up in *Bildung* in this fundamental sense. Of *Bildung* in this sense, Gadamer writes that it "is not only . . . the process which produces the historical raising of the mind to the universal, but it is at the same time the element within which the educated man (*Gebildete*) moves" (T&M, 15). Thus what is above translated as the "pre-given body of material" that the *Gebildete* must appropriate is more literally translated as the "pre-given substance" (*vorgegebene Substanz*), within which the *Gebildete* moves and to which he or she returns again and again.

While Gadamer follows Hegel in this account of *Bildung* and in the usage of the term "substance" in this way, he parts company with him in the end. As Weinsheimer explains:

> To be only in return means that the traveler, recalling
> Heraclitus, is different from and more than when he set
> out. But, to reverse the Heraclitean maxim he can *only* go
> home again: the "more" that he is upon return is that he is
> more fully himself. . . . Further, to *be* only in return means
> that the spirit *is* only insofar as it keeps returning. . . .
> Gadamer departs from Hegel in that he envisions no end
> point where the movement of alienation and return can
> cease in a total self-appropriation. [GH, 70–71]

As Gadamer states: "Hegel's answer cannot satisfy us, for Bildung [*sic*] as the movement of alienation and appropriation perfects itself for Hegel in a complete mastery of substance (*Bemäch-tigung der Substanz*), in the dissolution of all objective being, which is first reached in the absolute knowledge of philosophy" (T&M, 15; translation modified by me).

Gadamer's objection to Hegel is later clarified in Part Two of *Truth and Method*. Hegel's claim to absolute knowledge is understood as knowledge "in which history would become completely transparent to itself and hence be raised to the level of a concept" (T&M, 268). It would occur in an act of total self-appropriation by absolute spirit, a "form of spirit that contains nothing more in itself that is alien, other, or in opposition" (PH, 114). However, this is to deny the Gadamerian thesis that "understanding (including self-understanding) is and always remains conditioned by its situation; and that this situation cannot be objectified or taken into account in such a way that its effects could be subtracted from the process of cognition" (GH, 11). As stated previously, one finds oneself "always already" in a situation or "always already" in the process of *Bildung*, so that one's under-standing or self-understanding is, as was amply detailed in chapter 1, always already a part of the event that is to be understood.

Gadamer continues this discussion of *wirkungsgeschichtliches Bewusstsein* and the necessity of the hermeneutical situation by returning to the notion of substance that had been developed in the previous part on *Bildung*. He writes: "All self-knowledge proceeds from what is historically pregiven, what we call, with Hegel, 'substance,' because it is the basis of all subjective thinking and conduct and hence both prescribes and limits every possibility of understanding any tradition whatsoever in terms of its unique histor-ical quality" (T&M, 269). The task of philosophical hermeneutics is not to master substance in this sense, for, as Gadamer states here, "Being historical means never dissolving into self-knowledge" (Y&M, 269). Rather the task of philosophical hermeneutics "can be thus characterized: it would have to retrace the way of Hegel's phenome-nology of spirit backwards" (T&M, 269). This task involves retracing the way backwards "until we show in all that is subjective the substan-tiality that determines it" (T&M, 269).[3]

Hegel's absolute spirit is not simply or primarily substance, but, as is well known, substance and subject at once. Hence Gadamer's retracing backwards is not only a retracing from subject back to substance, but, as a consequence of the denial of the possi-bility of absolute knowledge, a retracing from absolute spirit back to objective spirit. Gadamer understands Hegel's theory of objective spirit as follows: "The thrust of the theory of objective spirit is that not the consciousness of the individual but a common and normative reality that surpasses the awareness of the individual is the foundation of our life in state and society" (RAS, 31). By his reading of Hegel's theory, therefore, objective spirit is directly parallel to and scarcely distinguishable from his own conception of tradition. Thus the retracing of the phenomenology of spirit involves for Gadamer a movement back from the substance and subjectivity of an absolute spirit back to the substantiality of tradition.

Clearly operative in this backward movement is Gadamer's notion of effective history as history that works itself out "beyond our willing and doing." Yet even more crucial is the consciousness of this effective history and how Gadamer conceives this consciousness in a manner quite different from Hegel. For Gadamer the most important feature of this consciousness is that it is finite. The consequence of this fact of human finitude is that the "historically effected consciousness is finite in so radical a sense that our being, effected by the whole of our history, essentially far surpasses the knowledge of itself" (T&M, xxii). Thus we return to one of Gadamer's most important theses, already explained in chapter 1, that *wirkungsgeschichtliches Bewusstsein* is more being that consciousness—a thesis that can now be seen to be obviously parallel to Gadamer's endeavor to retrace subjectivity back to Hegelian-Gadamerian "substance."

The major challenge facing Gadamer in his defense of the thesis on the limits of *wirkungsgeschichtliches Bewusstsein* lies within the experience of this consciousness itself. Although it can be successfully shown that this consciousness is part of and an effect of effective history, Gadamer concedes: "However much we say that it is itself within the effect, as consciousness it is of its essence to be able to rise above that of which it is consciousness" (T&M, 306). As Weinsheimer explains:

> It is not only consciousness of a historical object but self-consciousness and self-understanding that the historian achieves in such a realization. But does not this self-consciousness imply that history no longer can have a direct effect on the historian but that everything is filtered and mediated through consciousness? . . . Hegel contends for this reason that history is an element of consciousness: history dissolves into the thought of it. [GH, 200]

Gadamer confirms this explanation and gives a nice characterization of the danger as he sees it, when he writes: "We are concerned with understanding effective-historical consciousness in such a way that the immediacy and superiority of the work does not disintegrate into a mere reflective reality in the consciousness of the effect, i.e. we are concerned to conceive a reality which is beyond the omnipotence of reflection" (T&M, 307).

Gadamer attacks the supposed omnipotence of reflection in at least two ways. One way, which is less crucial for the interest at hand, is to point to earlier historical developments from Aristotle, Bretano, Heidegger, and others that indicate a nonobjectifying form of reflection that distinguishes it from reflection as understood in German Idealism.[4] The other way is to argue that, again as has been seen earlier, historical understanding is an event or happening. As Gadamer explains:

> The issue here is not simply that a nonobjectifying consciousness always accompanies the process of understanding, but rather that understanding is not suitably conceived at all as a consciousness of something, since the whole process of understanding itself enters into an event, is brought about by it, and is permeated by it. The freedom of reflection, this presumed being-with-itself, does not occur at all in understanding, so much is understanding conditioned at every moment by the historicity of existence. [PH, 125]

Gadamer's view of how understanding is always conditioned by the historicity of human finitude comes through most clearly in his conception of experience. For him, the crucial fact concerning the analysis of *wirkungsgeschichtliches Bewusstsein* is that it has the structure of an experience. However, his conception of experience differs from Hegel's, since, according to Gadamer, Hegel understands experience not in terms of its process but rather in terms of its result. Experience for Hegel is an experience that consciousness has of itself through its encounter with the other and involves a reversal or transformation of consciousness when it recognizes itself in what is alien and different. For Gadamer this aspect of the description of experience has something true about it, as Grondin explains: "The hermeneutical 'experience' is . . . nothing other than the process of the furthering of the object which calls forth the enrichment of the subject. On both sides something 'new' is called into life" (HW, 56). However, Gadamer objects when experience leads to a self-knowledge that no longer has any aspect of difference or otherness, but a "presumed being with itself." The result of this experience is not further experience, but knowledge, actually absolute knowledge, which is why for Hegel "the dialectic of experience must end with the overcoming of all experience" (T&M, 319).

For Gadamer, in contrast, the emphasis is not upon the result of experience or the end of the experience, but upon the process of experience. If anything is infinite, it is the actual process of experience and not the knowledge that would be at the end of the process. Thus the end of experience is further experience, and the hermeneutical requirement is to be oriented toward the new experience, to be open to it. Gadamer's difference with Hegel on the nature of experience becomes clear when he writes: "The dialectic of experience has its own completion not in conclusive knowledge but instead in that openness to experience that is brought into play by experience itself" (T&M, 319). Experience is being understood in this contrast as referring "chiefly to painful and disagreeable experiences" (T&M, 319), to disappointments of expectations that result from experience acquired without being sought out or intended. Therefore the experienced human being is someone who has learned "not any particular thing but rather the uncertainty of all plans and predictions, the frustration of all attempts to control or close off the future, and the disappointment of all aspirations to comprehend in a single concept, however inclusive, the infinite process of experience" (GH, 204–5).

Bildung, too, it can be seen, is another expression of the very same process within which finite human beings are situated. Consequently openness to the process of *Bildung* is similarly the most important requirement for the carrying out of *Bildung*. If the conceptual tie between *Bildung* and the acquisition of potency is recalled, this might suggest an attitude of openness toward the potency of the event of *Bildung* itself with a concomitant "letting happen" of the "truth" of the event. However, another interpretation of the same phenomenon might also be that the attitude of openness is itself a potency that is acquired. The open human being is the undogmatic and humble person who knows that tradition is a great teacher and that there is a need for its education. Under either interpretation, however, or even under both together, the experienced human being (*Erfahrene*) is the developed and educated human being (*Gebildete*).

Both the experienced human being and the educated human being are experienced in and educated by human finitude or, to use the earlier phrase, "the historicity of existence." Consciousness of effective history or *wirkungsgeschichtliches Bewusstsein* is the conscious openness to experience that is "the experience of human finitude" and "of one's own historicality." It is this finitude and this historicality that limit the omnipotence of reflection that could only be achieved by an infinite spirit. And with the limitation of reflection, the ontological role of tradition as the event within which consciousness is situated is secured in its full importance as the medium and substance of both *Bildung* and experience.

Retracing the *Phenomenology* Backward II

In the period immediately before his debate with Gadamer, Jürgen Habermas is involved in what can be interpreted for the purposes of comparison as his own retracing effort with respect to Hegel. The primary record of this effort is not contained in *Knowledge and Human Interests*, but in an earlier essay, "Labor and Interaction: Remarks on Hegel's Jena *Philosophy of Mind.*" The subtitle of the essay conveys the direction of the retracing. Habermas wishes to retrace not a single part of the *Phenomenology* back to another, but the whole *Phenomenology* back to an earlier conception of it that he finds to be more valuable for social theory today. Concerning Hegel's lectures on the philosophy of nature and of mind that were held in Jena during 1803–4 and 1805–6, Habermas writes: "Language, labor, and action in reciprocity were not only stages in the formative process of spirit, but also principles of its formation itself" (T&P, 161–62). Of the thesis of his essay, he states: "A radicalization of my thesis would read: it is not spirit in the absolute movement of reflecting on itself which manifests itself in, among other things, language, labor, and moral relationships, but rather it is the dialectical interconnections between linguistic symbolization, labor, and interaction which determine the concept of spirit" (T&P, 142–43).

Of the three dialectical forms of mediation and construction, interaction plays the most central role in Habermas's argument. Hegel distinguishes himself from Kant in conceiving of the identity of self-consciousness not as originary (*ursprünglich*), but as developed (*geworden*) (T&P, 156–57). Moreover he differs from Fichte in not conceiving of this process of development as an act of solitary reflection of self-consciousness prior to its other accomplishments. Rather the experience of self-consciousness "results from the experience of interaction, in which I learn to see myself through the eyes of other subjects" (T&P, 145). Thus the process of self-formation or *Bildungsprozess* depends upon the achievement of mutual recognition by different selves who can each say "I" and yet recognize one another. Within this interactive process, "spirit is not the foundation (*Fundamentum*) underlying the subjectivity of the self in self-consciousness, but rather the medium *within* which one 'I' communicates with another 'I', and *from* which, as an absolute mediation, the two mutually form each other into subjects" (T&P, 145). Therefore the process of interaction for Hegel is interpreted by Habermas to be a process of socialization—not, however, of pregiven individuals but of individuals themselves produced within the medium of spirit or consciousness.

Moreover, the attainment of mutual recognition through social interaction is neither simple nor straightforward: Hegel speaks of the struggle (*Kampf*) for recognition. The different selves originally oppose one another and suppress interaction; therefore they have to be reconciled with one another in order for mutual recognition to occur. The necessity of overcoming the suppression of social interaction is what makes the entire process a dialectical one, as Habermas explains:

> What is dialectical is not unconstrained intersubjectivity itself, but the history of its suppression and reconstitution. The distortion of the dialogic relationship is subject to the causality of split-off symbols and reified logical relations— that is, relations that have been taken out of the context of communication and thus are valid and operative only behind the backs of the subjects. The young Hegel speaks of a causality of destiny. [T&P, 148]

In an early fragment, *The Spirit of Christianity*, Hegel develops the notion of a causality of fate while explaining the pathway of reconciliation for criminals with respect to the encompassing moral community. Criminals place themselves above the position of the total community through their criminal acts and cause a hardened opposition to themselves—a causality of fate—that can be overcome only through a longing on the part of both parties to restore the lost unity through a dialogic relationship. In the Jena lectures, the same pattern is discerned, only over a broader context than punishment. The struggle for recognition is seen as a general struggle of life and death that the combatants wage until their abstract sense of self-assertion that seeks to assert their singularity into a totality is overcome by a willingness to interact on the basis of "mutual recognition—namely on the basis of the knowledge that the identity of the 'I' is possible solely through the identity of the other who recognizes me, and who in turn is dependent upon my recognition" (T&P, 149; McCarthy's translation).

Interaction is only one of the dialectical forms or media through which the subject is formed for Hegel in the Jena period; the other media are language and labor. The dialectic of language is regarded as the achievement by linguistic symbols of the power to represent the world, to make "present something that is not immediately given through something that is immediately given, but which stands for something other that itself" (T&P, 153). With respect to labor, instruments occupy the same intermediary role as symbols. The tool is "that which is general as against the ephemeral moments of desire and enjoyment" (T&P, 154); it retains "the rules according to which the domination of natural processes can be repeated at will" (T&P, 154). However, the tool does not mediate between the subject and the world in the same manner as the symbol; the dialectic of labor "begins not with the subjection of nature to self-generated symbols, but, on the contrary, with the subjection of the subject to the power of external nature" (T&P, 154).

In point of fact, all three of the processes of language, labor, and interaction are heterogeneous, which "raises the question of the unity of the self-formative process, that is, of the relation of the different media" (CTJH, 32). The medium of language only exists as the language of a people, as the expression of a cultural tradition; as such, it is a presupposition for social and moral interaction. It is also a presupposition for labor, which "is embedded within a network of interactions, and therefore dependent on the communicative boundary conditions that underlie every possible cooperation" (T&P, 156).

There remains the relationship of labor to interaction, which is also the title of Habermas's essay. Concerning this relationship, Habermas states:

> Hegel links together labor and interaction under the view-
> point of emancipation from the forces of external as well
> as internal nature. He does not reduce interaction to labor,
> nor does he elevate labor to resolve it in interaction; still,
> he keeps the interconnection of the two in view. . . . The
> result of emancipation by means of labor enters into the
> norms under which we act complementarily. [T&P, 161]

The way that labor enters into legal norms comes from individuals recognizing each other as the owners of possessions that are produced by labor. In the rules that govern proprietorship there arises an institutionalization of the reciprocal exchange of products that is at the same time an institutionalization of the reciprocal recognition of legal persons. The "institutionalization of ego-identity, the legally sanctioned self-consciousness, is understood as a result of *both* processes: that of *labor* and that of the *struggle for recognition*" (T&P, 160).

Hegel did not persist in this independent but interconnected treatment of labor and interaction, or in the threefold, heterogeneous dialectics of language, labor, and interaction. The dialectic of master and slave in the *Phenomenology* maintains a similar treatment of labor and interaction, but already this dialectic is treated as a stage in the manifestation of absolute spirit. Moreover, already in the Jena lectures there is an absolute identity between nature and absolute spirit, because spirit overcomes its apparent otherness or alienation from nature. Nature is thereby being treated not as an object (*Gegenstand*) but as an adversary (*Gegenspieler*) "with which interaction in the mode of that between subjects is possible" (T&P, 163).

For the dialectics of language and labor described earlier, by contrast, a relationship forms "between a knowing or acting subject on the one hand, and an object as the epitome of what does not belong to the subject on the other" (T&P, 163). Only with respect to the dialectic of love and conflict is the movement on the level of intersubjectivity, and the goal of the movement is reconciliation with other subjects and not the objectification or appropriation of external nature. Habermas argues that the "idealistic sublation of the distinction between objects as objects (*Gegenstände*) and as adversaries (*Gegenspieler*) makes possible the assimilation of these heterogeneous models: if interaction is possible with nature as a hidden subject in the role of the Other, then the processes of externalization and appropriation formally match those of alienation and reconciliation" (T&P, 164). Under the idealistic presupposition of a process of self-formation of absolute spirit, the three dialectics of language, labor, and interaction only appear to be heterogeneous and the unity of the process is no longer secured by the interrelationship of labor and interaction, but rather by the self-reflection of the absolute in coming to the consciousness of itself.

Consequently Habermas criticizes Hegel's philosophy of the absolute, but for reasons that are quite different from Gadamer's. Gadamer criticizes the self-reflection of the absolute for the mastery of substance (*Bemächtigung der Substanz*) with respect to objective *spirit*; his purpose is to defend the substantiality of tradition against the claim of omnipotence from reflection. If the same vocabulary is adopted and admittedly extended with respect to Habermas, he criticizes "the mastery of substance" with respect to objective *nature*; his purpose is not, however, so much to defend the materiality of nature as the materiality of the whole process of the development of spirit. The materiality of the *Bildungsprozess* is secured, according to Habermas, by the maintenance of the distinction between labor and interaction from Hegel's Jena philosophy that is later relegated and collapsed in the *Phenomenology* and other writings. But reflection is not criticized for the overambitiousness of its claims with respect to history and tradition, rather only for its failure to distinguish between objectivity and intersubjectivity, between appropriation and reconciliation.

Indeed, despite the fact that Habermas criticizes Hegel's characterization of the *Bildungsprozess* as a process of self-reflection of the absolute and seeks to return to a materialist reconstruction of this process in terms of the interconnection between labor and interaction, he at the same time preserves the concept of self-reflection and attributes to it a crucial role in his major work of this period, *Knowledge and Human Interests*.[5] The combination of the critique of idealism together with the preservation of one of its most central concepts presents a certain tension in Habermas's thought and offers one of the sources for Gadamer's reply to his criticisms of philosophical hermeneutics. Consequently it will be necessary to examine more closely Habermas's conception of self-reflection as it appears in his treatment of Freudian psychoanalysis in *Knowledge and Human Interests*.

Self-Reflection and Psychoanalysis in *Knowledge and Human Interests*

Habermas's own attempt to develop the proper interrelationship between labor and interaction and to preserve the heterogeneous character of language, labor, and interaction is presented in *Knowledge and Human Interests*. The materialist intention present in Hegel's early distinctions among the heterogeneous processes of labor, language, and interaction is conveyed by the three knowledge-constitutive interests that Habermas seeks to establish through a dialectical mode of presentation: first, an interest in instrumental or purposive-rational action that seeks technical control; second, an interest in communicative action that seeks mutual understanding; and third, an emancipatory interest that seeks freedom from pseudo-natural constraints. The final interest is considered to be the underlying interest of a critical theory of society that both analyzes the interrelationships of labor and interaction in the process of self-formation of society and criticizes the forms of domination present in these interrelationships. It is not adverse to, but rather actively advocates, important "normative goals of enlightenment—self-emancipation through self-understanding, the overcoming of systematically distorted communication, and the strengthening of the capacity for self-determination through rational discourse" (CTJH, 213).

One of the two major figures in *Knowledge and Human Interests* who play the most prominent roles in contributing to this conception of a critical theory of society is Sigmund Freud.[6] As Thomas McCarthy explains:

> Habermas sees the specific advantage of incorporating Freud's ideas into historical materialism in the possibilities this opens for reconceptualizing "power" and "ideology" and for clarifying the status of a critical science. Institutionalized power relations, like individual neuroses, bring about a relatively rigid reproduction of behavior that is removed from criticism. . . . Repressed motives for action are excluded from communication and directed into channels of substitute gratification. These symbolically redirected motives are the forces that dominate consciousness by legitimating existing power relations. In this sense, institutions of power are rooted in distorted communication, in ideologically imprisoned consciousness. . . . Within the framework of a historical materialism that has incorporated Freud in this way, it is possible, Habermas believes, to clarify the status of the critical science that reconstructs the self-formative process of the species and to explicate the ideas of reason and of an emancipatory interest in reason that underlie it. The forms of the manifestation of consciousness that were, according to Hegel [in his post-Jena thought], successfully overcome in the absolute movement of mind, can now be grasped as rigidified forms of life, constellations of power and ideology that have been undermined by the development of the forces of production. [CTJH, 85-86]

Habermas claims of psychoanalysis that it is "the only tangible example of a science incorporating methodical self-reflection" (K&HI, 214) that overcomes such rigidified forms of life.

A somewhat artificial means of exposition will be employed in explicating the treatment of psychoanalysis in *Knowledge and Human Interests*. The three normative goals for critical theory quoted above from McCarthy's *The Critical Theory of Jürgen Habermas*—self-emancipation through self-understanding, the overcoming of systematically distorted communication, and the strengthening for the capacity for self-determination through rational discourse—will be treated separately in order to divide three different aspects or dimensions of Habermas's treatment of psychoanalysis. The first goal will indeed accord with the model of self-reflection as emancipation. However, the second goal will correlate with the conception of psychoanalysis as depth hermeneutics, and the third goal with Habermas's views on the "working alliance" between therapist and patient. Both the division of goals and the separation of Habermas's treatment of psychoanalysis into these dimensions will appear and are artificial in view of his unified conception of critical theory and of psychoanalysis. But these measures will later prove useful in the next chapter when an evaluation is made of criticisms from Gadamer concerning Habermas's conception of self-reflection as it appears in *Knowledge and Human Interests*. In particular, the distinction between self-emancipation and the strengthening for the capacity for self-determination will allow criticisms of the former to be both admitted and yet deflected as criticisms of the latter goal.

Habermas is influenced in his interpretation of psychoanalysis as a form of "depth hermeneutics" by Alfred Lorenzer, above all by Lorenzer's ideas that later appeared in the book, *Sprachzerstörung und Rekonstruktion*. Especially useful in this context is the discussion of the classic case of little Hans. Hans was a five-year-old boy who had an intense phobia of horses. The immediate precipitating cause of the phobia was the fall of a big, heavy horse. Lorenzer describes the process of interpretation involved in this case in terms of a five-step operation:

> First Step of Operation: The analyst recognizes (to stay with the horse/father example) that the meaning of the word "horse" is not correct; he concludes this from the behavior of the patient.
> Second Step of Operation: The analyst takes the opportunity to note that the patient transfers his anxiety from the horse over to him. Therefore he recognizes
> Analyst = Horse
> on the basis of the following equivalences:
> a) Scene with the analyst = Scene with the horse in the anxiety situation
> b) Ego of the patient before the analyst = Ego before the horse
> Third Step of Operation: The analyst is able to complicate the situation further by adding to the situation when he has the opportunity the further scenic constellation
> Analyst = Father
> In condensed form the equivalences now read like this:
> Analyst = Father
> Analyst = Horse
> which produces the conjecture

Horse = Father

The Fourth Step of Operation ought to reconstruct the
lost or missing situation by means of the entire framework
of meaning which has been mutilated through repression.
The conjecture

Horse = Father

is made good on by getting the interpretation of the horse
scene to force out the missing scene. This will then
produce:

Scene with the horse = Scene with the father

which makes clear that:

Horse = Father

The Fifth Step of Operation devolves upon the analyst and
the patient as the conclusion and occurs as soon as the ego
of the patient has achieved full and undiminished access to
the meaning of the symbols "Father" and "Horse." Now
the ego is capable of pushing forward its misguided formation of symbols and in accord with the common linguistic
behavior to also make up for it. There results (by the ideal
type of completion):

Horse = Horse
Father = Father
Analyst = Analyst

The displacement of language is put in order. The privatized language is dissolved and the language of the patient
is brought into congruence with the common language.[7]
[S&R, 135–36; translation is my own]

In this case Hans cannot publicly express his wish that his
father die. Therefore this desire becomes excluded or, to use a more
socially oriented term, excommunicated from the realm of publicly
acknowledged symbols. Instead a privatized wish associated with the
fall of a dead horse takes its place. Publicly licensed or approved need
expressions are distinguished from privatized, nonlicensed, or disap-
proved need expressions by the social force of repression that
excludes certain need expressions from public expression. Hans uses
a wish that is publicly licensed to disguise a wish that neither he nor
his family can admit. The disguised wish has therefore been
"desymbolized" and needs correspondingly to be "resymbolized"[8]
through the interpretation of the scene of original repression or
excommunication. In this way language can again, to use Lorenzer's
phrase, be "put in order."

The social force of repression is an expression of social power
in the form of a relationship of domination between one individual or
group and another. Psychoanalytic interpretation can make the indi-

vidual aware that distortions of language usage are signs of inferior social power. As distortions of language usage are signs of differentials in social power, so the restoration of correct language can be a first step toward overcoming the power relationship. Psychoanalysis that proceeds in this way can achieve the second normative goal of critical theory—the overcoming of systematically distorted communication, because it is a form of "depth hermeneutics" that does not interpret linguistic symbols, but distortions in their usage and differentials in social power.

Psychoanalysis is for Habermas, moreover, the best scientific exemplar of the first goal of critical theory, self-emancipation through self-understanding, because of the power it attributes to self-reflection. In "translating symbols from a mode of expression deformed as a private language into the mode of expression of public communication" (K&HI, 228), the analyst "reveals the genetically important phases of life history to a memory that was previously blocked, and brings to consciousness the person's own self-formative process" (K&HI, 228). The analyst "*reconstructs* what has been forgotten . . . from . . . dreams, associations, repetitions" (K&HI, 230), while the patient, "animated by the constructions suggested by the physician as hypotheses, *remembers*" (K&HI, 230).

The reconstruction of what has been forgotten depends upon the analyst's capacity for "scenic understanding." "Scenic understanding" is a term employed by Lorenzer to refer to the fact that what is to be interpreted is a complete scene representing a total social interaction. The symbols that are interpreted in Hans's case, for example, are not to be understood simply as "father" or "child" but require the general characterization of the entire scene to give them their concreteness. An "understanding father" stands in scenic constellation with a "loving child"; a "punishing father," in scenic constellation with a "misbehaving child." When a symbol is embedded into such a definite scenic constellation and this constellation is repressed, Lorenzer refers to it as a "cliché" (*Klischee*) (S&R, 113). Through repression the cliché becomes stereotyped to the specific scenic constellation that produced it, and the pattern of the entire scenic interaction becomes evoked whenever the cliché is unconsciously called to mind.

The result is Lorenzer's interpretation of the famous Freudian concept of the "compulsion to repeat." The analyst makes special use of this compulsion in stimulating a transference neurosis on the part of the patient. The analytic situation in general promotes the development of conditions of transference or, in Lorenzer's vocabulary, the possibility that the neurotic will repeat his or her "scenic behavior" in interaction with the therapist. Of the analytic situation, Habermas writes:

> First it weakens defense mechanisms through the reduction of conscious controls (by relaxation, free association, and unreserved communication), thus reinforcing the need to act. At the same time, however, it makes these repetitive reactions run idle in the presence of a reserved partner who suspends the pressure of life. Thus these reactions react back upon the patient himself. [K&HI, 231–32]

The result is that "the patient forces the physician into the role of the conflict-defined primary reference person" (TCC, 119). The physician can now "interpret the transference situation as a repetition of early childhood experiences; he thus can construct a dictionary for the hidden idiosyncratic meanings of the symptoms" (TCC, 119).

If the analyst reconstructs, the analysand remembers. Of this remembering, Habermas claims that "for the patient's remembering to be therapeutically successful, it must lead to the *conscious* appropriation of a suppressed fragment of life history" (K&HI, 251). The act of conscious appropriation is considered by Habermas to be an act of self-reflection of a subject that becomes aware that it is returning to itself and an earlier part of its history. Freud writes of the determination of the patient to "work through" resistances for the purposes of understanding "internal foreign territory" and of altering symptomatic behavior. Habermas calls this determination the "passion for critique" and refers to critique itself as the power to dissolve false consciousness: "Critique would not have the power to break up false consciousness if it were not impelled by a *passion for critique*" (K&HI, 234).

The false consciousness from which the psychoanalytic subject is seeking emancipation is for Habermas of the same kind as produced by Hegel's causality of fate; namely, a "causality of split-off symbols and reified logical relations—that is, relations that have been taken out of the context of communication and are valid and operative only behind the backs of the subjects" (T&P, 148). Hence, "the causal connections do not represent an invariance of natural laws but an invariance of life history that can be dissolved by the power of reflection" (CTJH, 201). In the act of self-reflection, the process of splitting-off is reversed so that the remembering of the patient, or the attainment of self-understanding, is at the same time an act of reappropriation of life history and self-emancipation away from pseudonatural constraints.

At the same time that self-reflection is given such a powerful role in this exposition of psychoanalytic practice, it is also, as the allusion to Hegel's causality of fate makes particularly clear, situated in a process of mutual social interaction.[9] More precisely, self-reflection is seen as the means for turning a misguided process of social self-formation into a successful one. While it may certainly appear artificial to concentrate now upon the social interactive aspects of this process and how they also serve to bring about change in the patient, this concentration will have the benefit of introducing previously neglected aspects of the process of psychoanalytic practice. In particular, the third normative goal for critical theory—the strengthening of the capacity for self-determination through rational discourse—will come more to the forefront of attention.

The psychoanlyst is able to make the reconstructions that the patient must remember only in virtue of interpreting several identifications that the patient has made with him or her. For the purpose of illustrating this point, the example of little Hans is somewhat poorly chosen, for Freud did not form a "working alliance" with Hans but only worked through the intermediary of his father. Nevertheless it is possible to reconstruct what those identifications are that are proposed by Freud on the basis of his other clinical experience.

The first interpretation of an identification is present in Lorenzer's second step of operation—"Analyst = Horse." The therapist is able to propose this equivalence, because he or she recognizes the earlier scenic constellation of the patient as it has emerged through the narration of dream materials and free association, and believes that this constellation is being repeated in the present therapeutic context of transference. The second interpretation occurs in Lorenzer's third step where the analyst interprets the patient as identifying the analyst with the patient's father. In this instance, the therapist interprets that the patient is transferring his feelings of anxiety toward his father over to the therapist and probably over to other significant persons in the patient's life. This leads the therapist to propose a third identification between horse and father whose purpose is to reveal the original scenic constellation with the father or the original cliché that is continuing to be repeated until the present time. The analyst's interpretation in this instance cannot be proposed on the strength of an immediate participation in a transference relationship, but only on the basis of the apparent interrelationships of the two transference situations already analyzed.

This final interpretation will indeed call for the patient to remember and reappropriate a lost fragment of life history, as was explained above under the theme of self-reflection. However, it will also call for a profound change in the "working alliance" between the therapist and patient. The interpretation exhibits the temporal structure of a past event that is being repeated continuously in the present circumstances. This event involves a scene of rigid and stereotypical behavior of a child in the face of a dominant authority figure of the past. Yet insofar as, among other reasons, the interpretation is merely proposed by the analyst without imposing the patient's involuntary acceptance, it is also hoped to be communicated that the present working alliance is importantly different from the past scenic constellation. It is not—again it is to be hoped—a relationship of domination, so that the passive and anxiety-ridden stance assumed by the patient in the past is no longer necessary or even possible, if the present interaction is to be successful. The patient must grasp that the present social situation calls for a response different from the original scenic constellation so that this cliché need no longer function as the only option for future behavior in situations of like circumstances. The goal of the working alliance must be an equality between the principals that is achieved by the patient freeing himself or herself from the transference situation under the encouragement of the analyst's interpretations.

Under this emphasis for psychoanalytic practice, what the patient overcomes is not only the pseudo causality of linguistic distortions but also a disturbance in the process of socialization. A new "social identity" becomes established, which rests upon the assumption of a definite role for a specific scenic constellation and also upon the assumption of other roles for different occasions since the process of socialization has successfully been resumed. Moreover the basis for a "personal identity" has also been achieved. For if the working alliance truly changes its character, then there is a posssibility for a continuity exceeding mere temporal succession within the roles that have been differentiated, and the patient will be able to identify within this continuity a personal self-formative process that constitutes a personal identity. Consequently the patient learns not only the commonly acknowledged meanings of "Analyst," "Father," and "Horse," but also acquires the capability to incorporate these meanings, together with a great many others, into a coherent individual narrative understandable to the analyst and to the others the patient encounters.

Thus the succesful resolution of the transference neurosis through the working alliance between patient and therapist should carry with it the strengthening of the capacity for self-determination on the part of the patient. However, this strengthening comes about precisely insofar as the patient does not return to the event of the original scenic constellation but participates equally in a new social situation with new individual potentialities. In other words, the working alliance is not intended to be a home-"coming" but rather a home-"taking of departure," since its very success depends upon its becoming differentiated from the initial home situation. Hence the form of the appropriation of the patient does not resemble Gadamer's description of *Bildung* as preservation but rather conveys Habermas's conception of *Bildungsprozess* as a process of development and enlightenment. If Freud says, "Where id was, there ego shall be," the famous statement may be reformulated to read, "Where a disturbed process of socialization and of personal self-formation was, there successful socialization and independent personal identity shall be."

Such a reformulation of Freud's famous proclamation must compete from the outset, however, with another possible candidate for reformulation from within the bounds of Habermas's own treatment of psychoanalysis. For the emphasis upon self-reflection as the means for overcoming the disturbance in the process of self-formation also makes it an obvious candidate for reformulation as well. In an earlier section of *Knowledge and Human Interests* on Fichte, Habermas writes that the "experience of reflection articulates itself substantially in the concept of a self-formative process" (K&HI, 197). In self-reflection the self "makes itself transparent to itself as action that returns into itself" (K&HI, 207), but this experience becomes emancipatory or truly transparent only when the self "becomes transparent to itself in the history of its genesis" (K&HI, 207). This achievement of transparency can easily be related to Freud's pronouncement in order to produce "where an unappropriated, unconscious part of life history was, there a transparent, conscious self shall be."[10]

A preference between these two alternative reformulations of Freud's formula will be indicated in the coming chapter and reiterated in the final chapter. However, one avenue for arguing against the acceptability of both formulas is to place in doubt the very importance of subjectivity, self-reflection, and a progressive development of socialization *überhaupt*. Gadamer explicitly argues against Habermas's employment of self-reflection in his treatment of psychoanalysis in their debate, and he has continually pointed to the limitations of subjectivity in the transmission or working out of tradition. In the coming chapter, his argument on the limitations of reflection will be reviewed and to a great degree supported, but a strong role for subjectivity and individual achievement will be insisted upon in spite of this defense.

3

Historical Situatedness—
Limitation or Enablement?

While Hegel's philosophy and the concept of *Bildung* are the occasion for a comparison between Gadamer and Habermas on the themes of historical belongingness and personal achievement, Gadamer's thesis on historical situatedness is the actual and prime concern for any attempt to develop a more equally important conception of personal achievement that is still compatible with other philosophical hermeneutical concepts. This thesis is the main vehicle employed by Gadamer in his criticism of Hegel. Moreover it is also in evidence in both his actual response to Habermas in their debate and in any criticism that can be constructed with respect to Habermas's conception of self-formative process in *Knowledge and Human Interests*. Therefore it would doubtlessly also be appealed to in reference to any conception of appropriation and education that includes a moment or aspect of individual achievement as equally primary or equally essential as the moment of historical belongingness.

In this chapter, it will be seen how Gadamer criticizes Hegel by means of his thesis of historical situatedness and how a critique of Habermas is also easily fashioned by the same means. However, Gadamer's thesis of historical situatedness will also be carefully probed for what it quite justifiably entails and where it is actually overstated. The consequences of its overextension are examined with respect to his view of the event structure of appropriation and education, and it is argued that there is room for a more formidable notion of individual achievement than Gadamer appears to allow.

This notion is developed not by stressing the limiting character of being situated in history, but rather the enabling potential of historical situatedness to develop the capabilities of personal achievement. This enabling capacity is indicated briefly through the discussion of yet another description of the process of education, the "sentimental education" of the Balinese depicted by Clifford Geertz in his essay about cockfights on Bali. In addition, a concept that originates from Habermas—"balance"—is introduced into the discusssion and modified in order to express a balance in the relationship between belongingness and achievement as well as a balance between the event and personal act of appropriation.

Historical Situatedness

If the two contrasting treatments of, on the one hand, *Bildung* and experience and, on the other hand, *Bildungsprozess* and self-reflection are compared, then it is easy to anticipate Gadamer's criticisms of Habermas's views. Insofar as the act of self-reflection involves for Habermas the making transparent of past history, this is an indication for Gadamer of a lack of appreciation for human finitude and human historicity. Consequently if not an omnipotence, then at least an overpotency of reflection is being advocated in spite of Habermas's materialist reformulation of Hegel's Jena philosophy. In other words, Hegel's *Phenomenology* is still being read forwards rather than backwards, as a progression of subjectivity rather than a rehabilitation of substance. Therefore Gadamer's response to Habermas's criticisms of the claim to universality of philosophical hermeneutics parallels to a great degree his earlier criticisms of Hegel.

Essential to Gadamer's critique of Hegel is his estimation of the importance of the event of effective history and of tradition. His claim against Hegel is that historical understanding is "conditioned at every moment" by historicity, that the event of history "enters into" understanding, "permeates" it, "brings it about." Thus for him the consciousness of effective history or *wirkungsgeschichtliches Bewusstsein* is not an achievement of the reflective surpassing of history, but rather the openness to experience that reveals human finitude and the awareness of being conditioned by history.

Gadamer's argument against Hegel, if it can be termed such, is that the "consciousness of being conditioned in no way removes the conditionedness itself" (T&M, 406–7). In the German original, the verb in this sentence is a Hegelian one, *aufheben*, that is also being denied: *hebt keineswegs auf.*[1] If the triple meaning of this verb—to preserve, to cancel, and to raise up or improve—is brought into play, then it is the second and above all the third meanings of this verb that are being denied. The first meaning, on the contrary, is being affirmed and actually underscored by Gadamer. To recall the discussion of *Bildung*, it is the role of preservation that is at stake for the understanding of philosophical hermeneutics. This claim can now be clarified by saying that it is conditionedness that is preserved and not removed by hermeneutical awareness or the consciousness of effective history.

This claim about hermeneutical consciousness is a restatement of the thesis of human situatedness in understanding, a thesis expressed by Weinsheimer as follows: "understanding (including self-understanding) is and always remains conditioned by its situation; and that this situation cannot be objectified or taken into acount in such a way that its effects could be subtracted from the process of cognition" (GH, 11). Stated in this manner, the thesis can and will also be employed in the debate against Habermas with respect to the conception of self-reflection in *Knowledge and Human Interests*. However, the precise repercussions of this thesis upon the claims of self-reflection will also be made more difficult to discern, because of an important and famous ambiguity in the notion of self-reflection that Habermas himself later noted. As McCarthy explains:

> On the one hand, taking Kant as his point of departure,
> Habermas attempts to revive and radicalize the idea of a
> *critique of knowledge*. In this context "self-reflection" means
> reflection on the subjective conditions of knowledge, on
> the "a priori constitution" of the facts with which the
> objectifying sciences deal, on the "synthetic achievements
> of the knowing subject" . . . . On the other hand, taking
> Marx and Freud as points of departure, Habermas
> attempts to develop the idea of a *critique of ideology* that
> aims at freeing the subject from his dependence on
> "hypostasized powers" concealed in the structures of
> speech and action. In this context "self-reflection" refers to
> a "dialectic that takes the historical traces of suppressed
> dialogue and reconstructs what has been suppressed," that
> brings to consciousness "those determinants of a self-form-
> ative process which ideologically determine a contemporary
> praxis and world view." [CTJH, 94]

According to McCarthy, it is self-reflection in the second sense that is difficult to square with Habermas's rejection of idealism. Of course it is also self-reflection in this sense that is most vulnerable to Gadamer's arguments about the limitations of reflection. A peculiar aspect of the debate between Gadamer and Habermas, however, is that Gadamer indeed argues against self-reflection in the second sense that it is finite and limited, but in order to establish the limits of "method," including the critique of knowledge, in comparison to the "truth" of the event of hermeneutical understanding. And Habermas defends the power of reflection not so much to insist on a self-transparency of an individual life history as to insure that knowledge can be granted an autonomy from its historically contingent conditions. Therefore the most crucial disagreement in the debate is between the claim of universality of philosophical hermeneutics, a consequence of its understanding of the event of understanding, and Habermas's claim to a general theory of the presuppositions and conditions of language and communicative action. As McCarthy summarizes:

> Gadamer's universalization of hermeneutics rests on a
> logical argument against the possibility of methodologically
> transcending the hermeneutic point of view: any attempt
> to do so is inconsistent with the very conditions of possi-
> bility of understanding: the linguisticality and historicity of
> human existence. Habermas's counterposition is an attempt
> to mitigate the radically situational character of under-
> standing through the introduction of theoretical elements;
> the theories of communication and social evolution are
> meant to reduce the context-dependency of the basic cate-
> gories and assumptions of critical theory. [CTJH, 193]

If this interpretation of the debate is correct, then the main points of contention between Gadamer and Habermas actually concern the scope of self-reflection in the first sense, despite the fact that the conduct of the debate begins by being about the limitations of self-reflection in the second sense. Therefore, inasmuch as this study deals with the concepts of appropriation and *Bildung* within the context of philosophical hermeneutics, it is not, as a consequence, directed to the major concerns of the debate. Rather it takes up the original source of concern for self-reflection in the second sense, a concern eclipsed by the dynamics of the actual debate. This concern is with "reflection on the specific formative history of a *particular* (individual or group) subject; its goal is a restructuring of the subject's own action-orienting self-understanding through liberation from self-deception" (CTJH, 95).

Concerning this sense of self-reflection, Gadamer's argument against Hegel on the power of reflection is of course pertinent. The thesis of historical situatedness is of great importance in philosophical hermeneutics, and it does and ought to carry considerable weight against the advocacy of a reflective overcoming of the past or the achievement of a total transparency. Nevertheless this thesis also needs to be distinguished from other formulations in *Truth and Method* that overstate and go beyond its very legitimate bounds. These formulations involve the concept of substance or of language as the fundamental form of *Bildung* and they involve not the verb "condition" (*bedingen*) but rather the verb "determine" (*bestimmen*). For example, in the Introduction, as was seen earlier, Gadamer writes: "The conceptual framework in which philosophy develops has always already captivated us in the same way the language we live in determines us" (T&M, xv). And, in a crucial sentence from Part Two, the task of philosophical hermeneutics is characterized thus: "it would have to retrace the way of Hegel's phenomenology of spirit backwards until we show in all that is subjective the substantiality that determines it" (T&M, 268).

Of course one way to deal with these passages is to argue that the verb or participle employed does not really mean "determine" after all. Perhaps what is actually intended is that the language in which we live "forms" our subjectivity, "preshapes" our conscious judgments and actions, guides us before we are ever aware of it and "beyond our willing and doing." Yet even if this is an acceptable rendering of the first usage of *bestimmen*, the second usage is more problematic. For the intent of the backward reading of Hegel's *Phenomenology* is to lead what is supposedly subject under the presupposition of absolute knowledge back to substance, to the pregiven event in which subjectivity or consciousness participates. Hence it is claimed both that subjectivity is not independent of the event and that it is even determined by Hegelian "substance" or Gadamerian tradition.

The consciousness of *Wirkungsgeschichte* enters into this context, for it can also be used to suggest that the dependency of subjectivity upon substantiality is not simply that of a necessary condition, but even that of a sufficient one. Grondin writes: "The known fact that history works (*wirkt*) in us constitutes the moment of *wirkungsgeschichtliches Bewusstsein*. This consciousness is less a consciousness of the kind and way in which history is effective—which of course it can also be—as the consciousness that effective history continuously and in an uneliminable (*unaufhebbare*) way *determines* us" (HW, 145; my emphasis). Indeed the translator of Gadamer's *The Idea of the Good in Platonic-Aristotelian Philosophy*, Christopher Nowell Smith, and the new translators of *Truth and Method* agree with Grondin on this point and render *wirkungsgeschichtliches Bewusstsein* not as historically effec-tive but as historically effec*ted* consciousness (IG, 1n).

Within the bounds of this admittedly restrictive perspective toward the themes of subjectivity and consciousness in Gadamer, the language of a subject-determining substantiality is not at all surprising, especially when the most rhetorical comments about the self-awareness of the individual being a flickering in the closed circuits of historical life are also called to mind. But even more impor-tant than the language is the belief operating behind Gadamer's attempted retracing of Hegel that makes the language necessary. For Gadamer believes that it is necessary to substantialize the subject above all in order to give the event of the happening of tradition its due. In other words, Gadamer writes of a subject-determining substantiality not so much in order to explain how the subject is determined as rather to reveal the way that history works itself out into the present.[2]

Both the claim that the subject is an effect of a larger event and the belief that subjectivity must be criticized and limited for the sake of the event are important obstacles to the development of a concep-tion of individual achievement that could complement historical situ-atedness within the event. Actually the belief is, if possible, the bigger obstacle for a conception of appropriation as both historical belong-ingness and personal achievement. For it is the belief that impels the conception of appropriation as the "action of the thing" and not "our action upon the thing," the view that appropriation is an event, a happening, a transmission *alone* and not an individual achievement. Hence it is this belief, rather than the more excessive claims that self-awareness is a flickering or an effect, that needs to be examined and, if possible, refuted.

Habermas's claims in *Knowledge and Human Interests* about the power of self-reflection can be employed as valuable and needed correctives against the claims of a subjectivity-determining effective history, but they are more likely to be an obstacle in regard to the belief that subjectivity must be criticized and limited for the sake of the event-character of history. When the power of self-reflection is so accentuated that it includes the capability to dissolve the effects of tradition, this belief of Gadamer is and can only be reinforced. In other words, the advocacy of this conception of self-reflection entails an opposition to both the subjectivity-*determining* and subjectivity-*conditioning* aspects of history, with the latter opposition being by far the more troublesome to concede.

Another, more promising strategy for dealing with Gadamer's important and underlying belief that subjectivity must be sharply constrained for the sake of the event can be uncovered through a response to yet another argument for the way that historical substantiality determines subjectivity. In his Introduction to an anthology on philosophical hermeneutics, Brice R. Wachterhauser proposes as a Gadamerian thesis that "history determines our possibilities of understanding" (H&MP, 9). Insofar as the word "possibilities" is included in this thesis, it is a weaker statement of determining in relation to subjectivity and yet also a more plausible and defensible thesis. Its primary claim is not that the past determines present historical consciousness, but rather that it limits historical understanding: "we can see how the past may *limit* the number of possible ways we can come to understand something but it does not lock us into a predetermined grasp of some issue" (H&MP, 9). Thus the thesis represents a limit whose nature is such that it is not meant to be overcome but recognized as a consequence of the finitude of historical understanding. Because we are finite historical beings, we are situated in an event that limits or determines the possible understandings we can have.

In this thesis the situatedness of historical understanding is appealed to in order to establish not the stark claim that subjectivity is effected by the handing down of tradition, but rather the familiar claim that human understanding is finite. However, the emphasis of the thesis is solely upon how the event of historical transmission is a limit to human understanding. In the context of the earlier discussion on *Bildung*, it underscores how the event is a potency that is to be acquired by being open to its possibilities, by letting it come to word in the present situation. It does not state—although of course it does not explicitly deny—that there is a potency of a quite different kind that might also be acquired in the hermeneutical situation. This kind of potency is a potency for subjective achievement that may be and indeed is *limited* by the historical situation, but also is *enabled* by the historical event as well.

Therefore the best response to this formulation of the argument of historical situatedness is not so much to challenge its conclusion as to claim that it is more important to indicate how the event of understanding makes a conscious and intended act of understanding possible than it is to insist upon how it serves as a limit. With this strategy in mind, an emphasis upon enablement offers itself for consideration in comparison to Gadamer's emphasis upon limitation.

Perhaps the most essential part of Gadamer's argument that the event of understanding is a limit to subjectivity is how we "always already" belong to what we understand: to language, to tradition, to history—in short, to the event of understanding. The function of a stress upon enablement, as opposed to limitation, is to suggest that as we become conscious of our historicity we also become conscious of being "always already" enabled in the sense that we have already been furthered in our self-development. Rather than its being primarily a matter of our being limited by the greater potency of the event of *Bildung*, we have been led by its potency to the acquisition of our own potency to appropriate language, tradition, and history ourselves. Thus whereas the emphasis upon limitation characteristic of Gadamer supports more of an oppositional relationship between the "infinitude" of substance and the "finitude" of subjectivity, the stress upon enablement allows instead for a complementary relationship between the enabling tradition and the enabled subject.

Of course Gadamer's conception of belongingness is not in and of itself antithetical to the enabling capability of the historical event. Weinsheimer writes: "The second nature of custom and tradition is actually the first insofar as through the latter one becomes more fully what one is" (GH, 80). Gadamer states even more forcefully: "To stand within a tradition does not limit the freedom of knowledge but makes it possible" (T&M, 324). However, this description of the *Bildungsprozess* of self-formation does not consider the complementary role that the subject may play in furthering its development itself. If we have always already been situated in language, in history, and in tradition, then a further aspect of our experience of historicity is that we have always already achieved within the event of history, insofar as we have carried out the working out of history.

Of course an undeniably prominent aspect of this experience is the possibility that we have been forced to be enabled, we have been made to achieve. Yet even if this more negative aspect of compliance is undeniably present, it is more an indication of other, more negative, experiences of achievement than it is grounds for the denial of the possibility of a positive experience of enablement and of self-initiated achievement. In other words, the consciousness of the process of education or self-formation can still be a conjunctive consciousness of both historical belongingness and personal achievement rather than one of belongingness as the recognition of the limitation of subjective action.

The Sentimental Education of the Balinese Cockfight

The positive experience of enablement is an important aspect of the process of self-formation described by Habermas, at least as I have described it in regard to the change in the working alliance between therapist and patient described in the chapters on psychoanalysis in *Knowledge and Human Interests*. The major difficulty in capitalizing on this point, however, comes from the fact that the emancipatory thrust of self-reflection toward complete self-transparency is an at least equally important aspect of the same process, so that it is difficult to "distill out" either aspect in its pure form. In addition, the successful resolution of the working alliance on the side of the patient is conceived as the overcoming of a previously disturbed process of socialization and personal self-formation. Consequently, another description of the role of enablement in education would be useful that did not originate with a failure in *Bildung* or be so immediately subject to Gadamer's criticisms on the basis of the thesis of historical situatedness.

Such a description of the enabling character of education is borne out, in my estimation, in a third description of *Bildung* not usually associated with the Gadamer/Habermas debate. In Clifford Geertz's essay, "Deep Play: Notes on the Balinese Cockfight," the cockfighters, as well as the entire spectatorship, are described as being involved in a process of education of their own. In Geertz's words, "Attending cockfights and participating in them is, for the Balinese, a kind of sentimental education" (IC, 449).

Of course it might seem, at least at first glance, to be an excursion into frivolity to delve into the practice of cockfighting on the island of Bali after discussing Western humanistic *Bildung* and the complexities of psychoanalytic practice. However, Geertz takes great pains to dispel any impression of abnormality in the comparison of the occidental "great" with the oriental "lowly."[3] He compares the two minutes and forty seconds of the Balinese cockfight (two twenty-second rounds with a two-minute intermission), if not to Greek tragedy, then at least to Shakespeare and *Macbeth*:

> If, to quote Northrup Frye again, we go to see *Macbeth* to
> learn what a man feels like after he has gained a kingdom
> and lost his soul, Balinese go to cockfights to find out what
> a man, usually composed, aloof, almost obsessively self-
> absorbed, a kind of moral autocosm, feels like when,
> attacked, tormented, challenged, insulted, and driven in
> result to the extremes of fury, he has totally triumphed or
> been brought totally low. [IC, 450]

The first important point established in Geertz's analysis of the cockfight is that it is not just a gambling sport but really a "status war"

(IC, 417) between cockfighters and their alliances of implicated relatives and neighbors. Cockfights with high stakes are for the Balinese males who participate in them occasions for "deep play." This phrase was originally used by Jeremy Bentham to refer to games with stakes so high that it was irrational for would-be participants to take part, but Geertz revises it to refer to games where "much more is at stake than material gain: namely, esteem, honor, dignity, respect—in a word, though in Bali a profoundly freighted word, status" (IC, 433). Because of the great financial loss that is incurred by a betting alliance if the cock should die, the true Balinese cockfighters are engaged in a struggle where each has "to lay one's public self, allusively and metaphorically, through the medium of one's cock, on the line" (IC, 434). Each cockfighter faces the immediate prospect of an "emotional explosion" of exhilaration or anguish while he is exposed unmercifully in a most public spectacle. Of such battles, war is made.

However, Geertz also recognizes that the cockfight is very profoundly unlike a war due to its lack of material consequences. *"But no one's status really changes"* (IC, 433), he insists. This fact prompts him to call the cockfight a philosophical drama in addition to a status war and to compare it to the work of art:

> Like any art form—for that, finally, is what we are dealing with—the cockfight renders ordinary, everyday experience comprehensible by presenting it in terms of acts and objects which have had their practical consequences removed and been reduced (or, if you prefer, raised) to the level of sheer appearances, where their meaning can be more powerfully articulated and more exactly perceived. [IC, 443]

Thus, as quoted above, the cockfight resembles not so much the war of ascendancy of the historical Macbeth as the artistic drama that depicts how any great leader may be brought low by his deeds.

While the practical consequences upon status have indeed been removed in the Balinese cockfight, this is not to say that either the cockfight or the work of art in general are without consequences for Geertz. In Gadamer's terms, it can be said that the cockfight *wirkt* or works or operates upon its participants and spectators by making them disquiet. As Geertz explains:

> The reason it is disquietful is not that it has material effects (it has some, but they are minor); the reason that it is disquietful is that, joining pride to selfhood, selfhood to

cocks, and cocks to destruction, it brings to imaginative
realization a dimension of Balinese experience normally
well-obscured from view. The transfer of a sense of gravity
into what is in itself a rather blank and unvarious spectacle, a commotion of beating wings and throbbing legs, is
effected by interpreting it as expressive of something
unsettling in the way its authors and audience live, or,
even more ominously, what they are. . . . A powerful
rendering of life as the Balinese most deeply do not want
it . . . is set in the context of a sample of it as they do in
fact have it. [IC, 444, 446]

The cockfight unsettles or disquiets its participants and onlookers
through its power to disclose to them what they are—perhaps not
literally are, but, "what is almost worse, of how, from a particular
angle, they imaginatively are" (IC, 446). The Balinese who opens
himself or herself imaginatively to what the fight of the roosters
discloses must learn a most unpleasant revelation.

Geertz describes "what the cockfight says" in terms of, as noted
above, a "sentimental education" or education of the emotions:

What the cockfight says it says in a vocabulary of sentiment—the thrill of risk, the despair of loss, the pleasure of
triumph. Yet what it says is not merely that risk is exciting,
loss depressing, or triumph gratifying, banal tautologies of
affect, but that it is of these emotions, thus exampled, that
society is built and individuals are put together. [IC, 449]

The "content" of the education or its "truth" with Heideg-
gerian and Gadamerian connotations is one that establishes itself
through "a chicken hacking another mindlessly to bits" (IC, 449);
namely, "the cockfight talks most forcibly about status relationships,
and what it says about them is that they are matters of life and death"
(IC, 447).

To interpret the cockfight in terms of such deep significance is
to treat it decidedly not as "only a game" or "play" in the sense of
Gadamer's phenomenological description, but as "more than a game"
or "a play" in the sense of Gadamer's description of Greek tragedy.
As the repeatability of the structure (*Gebilde*) of the play allows it to
operate, work out its effective history, so for Geertz does the cockfight have the status of "a paradigmatic human event" (IC, 450). It is
an origin of Balinese culture and history, comparable to, as Geertz
observes, the mass festivals at the village temples and the ceremony
consecrating a Brahmana priest.

Geertz writes of the paradigmatic event of the cockfight in words that are compatible to the utmost with the event character of *Wirkungsgeschichte* in *Truth and Method*:

> Yet, because ... that subjectivity does not properly exist until it is thus organized, art forms generate and regenerate the very subjectivity they pretend only to display. Quartets, still lifes and cockfights are not merely reflections of pre-existing sensibility analogically represented; they are positive agents in the creation and maintenance of such a sensibility. [IC, 451]

However, even if subjectivity is not viewed as an independent agency over and against the cockfight, the paradigmatic character of the event is not used to limit or dismiss a more active conception of the sentimental education that the Balinese undergoes. Geertz writes rather in terms of enablement: "The cockfight enables the Balinese ... to see a dimension of his own subjectivity" (IC, 450). In this way the sentimental education is viewed in personal terms as an action of the individual Balinese as well as in historical terms as a paradigmatic event of cultural transmission.

Geertz concludes: "In the cockfight, then, the Balinese forms and discovers his temperament and his society's temper at the same time" (IC, 451). We can note here that, as a description of the *Bildung*, it describes a process of self-formation as both of ("discovers") and by ("forms") the self, whereas the emphasis in Gadamer's conception of *Bildung* falls above all upon how the subject is the object of the process. Moreover the conclusion is intended to extend to both the cockfighter who participates in the event and the spectator who watches it, for each is both forming and being formed by it. And, in contrast to the description of self-reflection by Habermas in *Knowledge and Human Interests*, both the cockfighter and the spectator make their discoveries not in order to overcome a pseudo-natural constraint or to compensate for a failure in development, but rather to learn for the first time or to have reinforced how their "society is built and individuals are put together."

This experience of mutual formation both of and by the self will be taken up more extensively—and more powerfully—in chapter 5 when the focus will be upon the young male spectator of the cockfight and upon what can be said about his aspirations from the perspective of Erik Erikson and his psychological/phenomenological writings. Furthermore, the role of consciousness in becoming aware of this mutual formation process will be taken up in the following chapter when a conception of consciousnesss inspired by an Erikson essay on an Ingmar Bergman film is developed and compared to Gadamer's *wirkungsgeschichtliches Bewusstsein*. For now it can be observed that the same mutual perspective toward self-formation is also in evidence in the chapter "The Virtues, the Unity of a Human Life and the Concept of a Tradition," in Alasdair MacIntyre's *After Virtue*. MacIntyre writes in agreement with Gadamer: "What I am, therefore, is in key part what I inherit, a specific past that is present to some degree in my present. I find myself part of a history and that is generally to say, whether I like it or not, whether I recognize it or not, one of the bearers of tradition" (AV, 221). He even states: "But the key question for men is not about their own authorship; I can only answer the question 'What am I to do?' if I can answer the prior question 'Of what story or stories do I find myself a part?' " (AV, 216). However, MacIntyre still has a place for the notion that we are at the same time "co-authors" in the stories of which we are a part: "Now I must emphasize that what the agent is able to do and say intelligibly as an actor is deeply affected by the fact that we are never more (and sometimes less) than the co-authors of our own narratives" (AV, 213).[4]

Balancing Achievement and Belongingness

This experience of personal *co*-authorship or of mutual forma-tion both *of* and *by* the self (both "forming" and "discovering") ought, in my estimation, to be incorporated in the tradition of philosophical hermeneutics and its description of the relationship of historical belongingness and personal achievement. In part the function of the introduction of the vocabulary of enablement is precisely to allow for this to happen without compromise to the important thesis of histor-ical situatedness. But in order to clarify further the relationship between belongingness and achievement, another concept from Habermas will be both introduced and, at the same time, modified.

This concept, *Balance*, is used by Habermas to explain the rela-tionship between social and personal identity as a "balance." The balance must be struck between the dangers of, on the one hand, being totally absorbed in the social identity we fall under and, on the other hand, being totally isolated and stigmatized by the personal identity we seek to express. Consequently, social and personal iden-tity stand in a "dialectical" relationship for Habermas, and both moments in the dialectic are to be balanced without either being subsumed. Ego identity is "grasped as the balance between the maintenance (*Aufrechterhaltung*) of both identities, the personal and the social" (KK, 131).

Although the concept of "balance" appears in an essay on sociological theories of socialization, the objective of the concept can be traced back to Habermas's essay on Hegel's Jena philosophy; namely, to develop a theory of socialization that is at the same time a theory of individualization and vice versa. The same concept also appears in a review essay by Habermas on a book by Klaus Heinrich:

> The material conditions of survival are therefore most intimately linked with those which are most sublime: the organic equilibrium is coupled with that precarious balance between separation and union in which, through the communication with others, the identity of each and every self must be established. [ZLS, 323]

I propose to employ the same metaphor of a balance between separation and union, only in a more hermeneutical context and in light of the attempt to establish that the history of *Bildung* that is understood by Gadamer in terms of the preservation of past tradition is at the same time a history of individual enablement and achievement.

The metaphorical structure that Gadamer gives to *Bildung* is, as we have seen, a very similar one of excursion and return. Indeed there is little to choose between the two structures. But the structure of excursion and return may afford a priority to the moment of return insofar as this moment completes the overall action. At least a priority is suggested by Gadamer, inasmuch as he states that the subject is only in return and that the return is actually and always a homecoming to tradition. The concept of balance between separation and union is intended to convey more of an equality between hermeneutical situatedness or union in the event of tradition and the personal achievement of separating oneself and becoming an individual within that tradition. Rather than saying that the subject is only in return with Gadamer, the subject is situated in a manner similar to Habermas in the balance between the maintenance of both hermeneutical situatedness or belongingness and the individual initiation required to form a personal identity.

The dangers that are to be averted under this modified concept of balance are, on the one hand, of being so totally absorbed in the working out of the event of tradition that Gadamer's pronouncement of being but a flickering in the closed circuits of historical life is (unfortunately) true and, on the other hand, of being totally isolated or, perhaps better, claiming total isolation from what is actually the necessary "substance" for the achievement of self-understanding. Hence belongingness, as expressed in some of its strongest formulations in *Truth and Method*, is not a goal of the balancing but an instantiation of the first danger where the process of *Bildung* is seen in terms solely of formation of the self. Moreover, self-reflection, understood as the total dissolution of the effects of past tradition and the attainment of pure transparency, is an instantiation of the second danger where *Bildung* might be understood as formation by the self alone.

It is important to add, however, that belongingness need not be understood solely in terms of limitation, but of course can and will be explained in terms of enablement of achievement as well. Similarly, self-reflection need not be understood as self-transparency, but may carry out different roles in the maintenance of the balance in a process of self-formation that is both of and by the self. Elements within Habermas's treatment of psychoanalysis point to how custom and tradition in the dynamics of family life may indeed be a first nature, but a first nature that disturbs the process of formation *by* the self and even prevents the self from *actively* becoming what one is. These are the elements that fall under the goal of what McCarthy describes as "the strengthening of the capacity for self-determination through rational discourse" and what is discussed here in terms of individual enablement through the strengthening of the capacity for personal achievement. Concerning the elements of Habermas's treatment of psychoanalysis that pertain to a disturbance in the process of socialization or of *Bildung*, self-reflection is not a goal in itself but a means to be employed in order to rectify the disturbance in the socialization process. Hence self-reflection can be a means of averting the first danger presented in the balance insofar as past life history is reflected upon in order to avoid its stereotypical repetition.

Gadamer's argument about the impossibility of transparent self-knowledge for human beings and the accompanying claim that all self-reflection is partial and imperfect can both be conceded, so long as a sufficient power of self-reflection remains for it to play its attributed role in the rectification of the socialization process. Moreover, becoming conscious need not be conceived, as it is in *Knowledge and Human Interests*, primarily as an overcoming of the pseudo-natural constraints of first nature. In the final chapter of this study, the conception of consciousness inspired by Erikson's writings will also be compared to Habermas's understanding of self-reflection.

This consciousness will involve above all a becoming aware of being enabled to achieve by one's first nature rather than being hindered by it. It will also be argued that this conception of consciousness, insofar as it does differ from self-reflection conceived as total self-transparence and dissolution of other-conditionedness, does not offer a target for hermeneutical attack, but rather a profound goal to be embraced in philosophical hermeneutics. This goal is, as has already been intimated above, not to overcome the effects of the event of effective history as described by Gadamer, but rather to articulate a different kind of consciousness than Gadamer's *wirkungsgeschichtliches Bewusstsein*, one that is able to allow for an equal role for human achievement.

Consciousness understood in this manner involves the personal and conscious appropriation of what is doubtlessly otherwise being appropriated in the unconscious transmission of tradition into the present. In other words, any dichotomy between the event of appropriation in tradition and the personal act of appropriating tradition is to be avoided in favor of a complementary relationship instead. Therefore the balance that is envisaged here may even be conceived in just as important a manner as lying between appropriation as a historical event and appropriation as a personal action. Indeed, another way of expressing the dangers to be avoided in the maintenance of the balance is that they are the consequences of viewing appropriation as, on the one hand, totally an event that is in the process of working itself out "beyond our willing and doing" and as, on the other hand, totally an individual action that needs no prior conditions. It may even be said, with Habermas, that the event of appropriation and the act of appropriating stand in a "dialectical" relationship where both moments are to be balanced without either being subsumed.

In order to elucidate further a conception of self-formation that is both of and by the subject, it is necessary to investigate more closely Habermas's concept of ego-identity, which plays the crucial role in the dialectical balance that he conceives between socialization and individualization. Moreover, this investigation will have the helpful effect of marking some of the important shifts in Habermas's thought since *Knowledge and Human Interests*. As is well known, he has changed his thought in important ways that have as a consequence that a total transparency of the self is no longer advocated. Moreover, what Habermas now claims concerning the achievement aspect of the self is placed within the context of developmental schemes for cognitive, linguistic, and interactive competences. The explication of these developmental schemes allows for a comparison with the famous eight-stage model of the life cycle from Erik Erikson and in this way a survey of some of his most important theoretical work as well. In particular, it makes possible the presentation of Erikson's views on the achievement of ego identity in a way that indicates both the similarities with and the differences from Habermas's account.

While this focus on the subject of personal identity may appear to be a shift to a more mundane level of achievement, such mundaneness may actually be a desideratum for the analysis. Until this point, the primary examples of achievement are the radicality of Habermasian emancipation and the profundity of Gadamerian openness to experience. While both are probably achievements of the greatest magnitude, the level of their sophistication creates the impression that achievement itself is difficult to "achieve." A comparison between Habermas and Erik Erikson on the theme of ego identity in the coming chapter will go great way in dispelling this impression and giving personal achievement its equal role in the balance with our belongingness to history.

4

Jürgen Habermas and
Erik Erikson on
Ego Identity

This chapter presents a comparison of the views of Jürgen Habermas and of Erik Erikson on the theme of ego identity. However, it must be emphasized at the outset that the comparison is neither exact nor pure. For Jürgen Habermas, ego identity is the *final* stage of a cognitive-developmental sequence beginning with natural identity, proceeding through role identity, and leading ultimately to ego identity. Ego identity in turn correlates very closely in its sequential position to the final stage in the development of interactive competence—Habermas's own concept and perhaps a more important concept overall in his developmental theories— which proceeds from preconventional through conventional to post-conventional levels. For Erik Erikson, by contrast, ego identity is involved above all in a *middle* stage of an eight-stage model of the life cycle of human beings. It is a developmental task for adolescents and is situated between an earlier stage of industry for later childhood and a later stage of intimacy for early adulthood. As a consequence, ego identity does not mean precisely the same developmental achievement for both thinkers.

Nor can the theories of identity formation for both Habermas and Erikson be so purely compared. For Habermas's theory of ego formation, his theory of the development of interactive competence, and many other developmental theories, the thought of Jean Piaget plays an exemplary role. In fact the progression to Piaget from

Habermas's earlier interests concerning the process of *Bildung* is stated clearly in the following quotation: "From Hegel through Freud to Piaget, the idea has developed that subject and object are reciprocally constituted, that the subject can grasp hold of itself only in relation to and by way of the construction of an objective world" (CES, 100). The new influence of Piaget upon Habermas is evident not only in how the relationship to external nature is explained but also in the form of the theory construction itself. Habermas distinguishes competence from performance as well as from any specific content of knowledge that is acquired. Thus competence involves for him a learning capacity that develops in the ontogenesis of the individual. Its existence is shown by rationally reconstructive sciences that reconstruct in a systematic fashion the intuitive knowledge (or know how) of competent subjects. Rational reconstruction explicates the "deep structures" or the rules by means of which cognitive operations occur or linguistic statements are made. It "attempts to make propositionally explicit through questioning and systematically ordered examples a prior, theoretically proved capacity to speak and act competently" (HDR, 239n). Moreover, "the formal nature of the rules ostensibly guarantees a level of generality sufficient to justify a claim to universal validity" (HDR, 239n).

For Habermas, the best exemplar of such a rationally reconstructive science of universal competences is Piaget's theory of cognitive development, which involves a progression from preoperational through concrete-operational to formal-operational thought. Concerning the sequence of stages, Habermas supplies the following quotation from his associates R. Döbert and G. Nunner-Winkler:

> The cognitive schemata of the individual phases are *qualitatively* distinct from one another, and the individual elements of a phase-specific style of thought are so related to one another that they form a *structured whole.* . . . The phase-specific schemata are ordered in an *invariant and hierarchically structured sequence.* This means that no later phase can be attained without passing through all those preceding it; further that in later stages of development the elements of earlier stages are transformed (*aufgehoben*) and re-integrated at a higher level; and moreover that for the sequence as a whole a direction of development can be specified. [CES, 220–21n]

Habermas seeks to present such progressive developmental sequences for the attainment of linguistic and interactive competences to complement Piaget's developmental account of the acquisition of cognitive competence. Moreover all three of these sequences fulfill for him the very important requirement of exhibiting the same *developmental logic* or formal pattern. Insofar as ego development occurs through the integration of inner nature into the universal structures of cognition, speech, and interaction, it too is the subject of such a developmental-logical pattern—the only caveat being that this sequence "highlights only the structural or—in a broader sense of the term—'cognitive' side of identity formation" and does not take up the other important aspect of "affective and motivational development" (CTJH, 339).

Erikson's description of the life cycle could be seen as a developmental-logical schema for affective and motivational development to supplement Habermas's cognitive account. However, if it is taken as such, even a cursory examination shows quite significant differences in his schema for the life cycle and in Habermas's developmental patterns. Erikson's description of the life cycle contrasts with the typical developmental schema from Habermas by having many more stages (eight versus either three or four), with the final four stages all falling under the more general Habermasian category of postconventional behavior. Moreover, especially these four stages are conceived less abstractly and formalistically. Instead of the development of the ability to perform new formal operations at a higher rational stage, they focus on the resolution of conflicts in the development of identity and later between intimacy and loneliness, generativity and self-absorption, and ego integrity and despair. Hence Habermas has objected against Erikson's description of the life cycle from the standpoint of the standards for a developmental logic that it is not sufficiently worked out:

> Finally advances have been undertaken from the side of analytic ego psychology (Erikson, Loevinger), but also following Mead, therefore with the means of symbolic interactionism. To be sure these approaches suffer from the fact that they do not convincingly distinguish the single developmental dimensions from one another, because the systematic point of view is missing which would allow them to project, to begin with hypothetically, a connection of independently developing competences. [VET, 191]

Habermas's concern for a rigorous developmental logic can be compared with a few of Erikson's own comments as to how his eight-stage model is to be understood. Concerning a chart of this model (and other models of his as well),[1] Erikson wishes to avoid the impression of a neatly achieved order and cautions against being taken too literally. He writes: "But a chart is only a tool to think with, and cannot aspire to be a prescription to abide by, whether in the practice of child-training, in psychotherapy, or in the methodology of child study" (EE, 136). Concerning another of his charts, he states: "The chart is now completed. To many it will seem an all too stereotyped way to account for the phenomena of early life" (C&S, 92n). Of Erikson's many different charts and many different kinds of charts, Robert Coles has written:

> He is trying to weave melodies, some that work and make
> good music, some that don't, and in fact are noise or
> worse. I suppose his "method" could be called contra-
> puntal—or in a way, Hegelian, in as much as it displays a
> certain dialectic, a certain progressive momentum. [EE,
> 137]

Therefore the chapter involves the inexact and "impure" comparison between the assets of more rigorous developmental schemata of theoretical explanation and the quite different virtues of, in Cole's words, the "contrapuntal melodies" of interpretive psychosocial patterns.

The Rational Reconstruction of
Personal and Social Identity

Jürgen Habermas's thought in the period between *Knowledge and Human Interests* and *The Theory of Communicative Action* is devoted not to the further elaboration of the theory of cognitive interests, but rather to the articulation of a complex, three-tiered research program. Thomas McCarthy describes the program in his Introduction to *Communication and the Evolution of Society*:

> The ground level consists of a general theory of communi-
> cation—as Habermas calls it, a universal pragmatics—at the
> next level this theory serves as the foundation for a
> general theory of socialization in the form of a theory of
> the acquisition of communicative competence; finally, at
> the highest level, which builds on those below it, Habermas
> sketches a theory of social evolution which he views as a
> reconstruction of historical materialism. [CES, xvii]

The theory of the acquisition of communicative competence is Habermas's own attempt to account for the development of an even broader range of learning capacities than Piaget. Inasmuch as communicative competence cannot be identified with linguistic competence alone, it also includes aspects of Piaget's cognitive competence, what Habermas introduces as interactive competence, and ego development as well. Ego development in turn is not viewed as an independent developmental process but rather as one parallel to and dependent upon cognitive, linguistic, and interactive development. For "each of these dimensions, and indeed only for these dimensions, a specific developmental-logically ordered universal sequence of structures can be given" (quoted in CTJH, 338).

By his own account "very tentatively," Habermas distinguishes four developmental-logical stages of ego development. In the first of these stages, the "symbiotic" phase, there are no clear indications of a subjective demarcation between the subject and the objects or persons of its surrounding environment. In the second stage, the "egocentric" stage, the child does make strides in differentiating itself from its environment, but the differentiation is not yet clear and an objective relationship is not attained. The third stage, the "sociocentric-objectivistic" phase, on the other hand, marks a decisive gain in the demarcating capability of the self. For here the child can now differentiate between persons and things, between language and its reference, between fantasy and perception, and between impulse and obligation. Yet in the final stage, the "universalistic" phase, the now adolescent can go beyond this to free himself or herself from "the dogmatism of the given and the existing" (CTJH, 340). The process by which this is done is more complicated and will demand our later attention in the specific case of practical reasoning, but it can be preliminarily described as the attainment of a "hypothetical" attitude toward the external and social regions, and a "reflexive" demarcation of the self from these regions.

The development of the ego may also be viewed from the more emphatically social-psychological perspective of identity formation, which of course is of greater interest to the theme of personal appropriation. From this perspective, Habermas suggests a three-stage pattern of identity formation: natural identity, role or conventional identity, and ego identity. Natural identity is attributable to the child simply in virtue of its body. In this respect plants and animals also have natural identities insofar as they not only have an identity for us as observers but also for themselves. The child goes on to acquire a role identity, however, by learning to locate itself within and to integrate itself into a social, symbolic world. The "unity of the person is formed through the internalization of roles that are tied in the beginning to concrete reference persons and later detached from them—primarily sex and generation roles that determine the structure of the family" (ZRHM, 23; in CTJH, 341). However, if the child first becomes a person by growing into the symbolic universe of the family, it becomes an adult or someone with an ego identity by growing out of it. The "ego identity of the adult confirms itself in the ability to construct new identities and simultaneously to integrate them with those overcome, so as to organize oneself and one's interactions in an unmistakeable life history" (EI, 11).

The transition from the role identity of the child and adolescent to the ego identity of the adult is of the greatest interest in this developmental pattern. It is explained in its greatest detail in an Introduction to an anthology of ego development that was written by Habermas and his two associates, Döbert and Nunner-Winkler:

> During this time the youth learns the important distinction between norms, on the one hand, and principles according to which we can generate norms, on the other. Such principles can serve as standards for criticizing and justifying existing norms; to one who judges on principle, all binding norms must appear as mere conventions. Among these, only *universal* norms let themselves be distinguished as moral, then only these assure the reciprocity of rights and duties of each vis-a-vis every one else. As soon as, however, in this sense the interactive reciprocity which is found in the role structure is itself raised to a principle, the ego can no longer identify with itself through particular roles and existing norms. It has to take into account that the traditionally accustomed forms of life prove themselves as merely particular, as irrational; therefore it must retract its identity, so to speak, behind the line of all *particular* roles and norms, and stabilize it only through the abstract ability to present itself in all situations as the one who can satisfy the requirements of consistency even in the face of incompatible role expectations and in the passage through a life-historical sequence of contradictory role systems. [EI, 10–11][2]

Within this process as it is here described, the role of tradition and accustomed forms of life is not to offer valuable contents (which in regard to moral theory are instead even and summarily labeled irrational!) to the growing adolescent, but rather to stimulate the develement of a higher level of moral reasoning and a higher level of reciprocity. Or, as stated later in the essay, "the adolescent borrows from the cultural tradition not only *contents*, but also the *constructive resources* (*Konstruktionsmittel*) for the building of an identity no longer bound to the family" (EI, 15).

The emphasis upon a transition in the capacity for moral reasoning is a strong indication of the competence whose development is being stimulated by the encounter with tradition: interactive competence as distinguished from linguistic and cognitive competence. Habermas designates the acquisition of interactive competence to be "the core of identity formation" (CTJH, 344). The attainment of the capacity for universal moral reasoning involves the completion of what is again a three-stage pattern of development from preconventional through conventional to postconventional behavior. Crucial to the attainment of the first transition is the introduction of the neutral attitude of the observer into the realm of interaction.

Crucial to the attainment of the second transition, already described above in the long quotation, is the introduction of hypothetical thinking into the interactive realm. With the appearance of "the capacity for formal-operational thought, the youth can acquire a certain distance from inherited roles, norms, and values; he can learn to place validity claims in question, to suspend recognition of them, and to treat them as hypothetical" (CTJH, 347). As a result, the "normative reality of society is no longer taken for granted" (CTJH, 349). Instead it may be made the subject of examination in a communicative discourse.[3] As McCarthy explains:

> What form of action occupies then the central place at
> level 3 that consensual role behavior occupied at level 2?
> Habermas's response is "communicative action": that type
> of action oriented to reaching understanding from which
> his universal pragmatics takes its start. The distinctive
> element here is the interpretive activity of the subject: "in
> role behavior the interacting parties can rely on an under-
> standing that has been previously secured through norma-
> tive integration; to the extent that this understanding is no
> longer unproblematic at the next level, it has to be
> replaced by the interpretive accomplishments of those
> involved." [CTJH, 349]

The goal of communicative action is a rational consensus to be brought about by the interpretive accomplishments of the subjects involved. Again, however, the past norms of a traditional consensus function, though in this instance considered as problematic and not as irrational, as the constructive resources out of which the rational consensus will be achieved.

This same perspective toward tradition as a catalyst or stimulant is evidenced in yet a further and final important developmental scheme. This scheme concerns the development of social or collective identity, and is of special importance in relation to Habermas's earlier work on socialization. For in that work there is, as we have seen in the previous chapter, the description of ego identity as a balance between personal identity and social identity. How is social identity now conceived in Habermas's competence-development approach and what affect does the developmental logic have upon the metaphor of balance between personal and social identity?

In the essay "Können komplexe Gesellschaften eine vernünftige Identität ausbilden?" (translated only in part as "On Social Identity"), a four-stage model for the development of social identity is proposed. The first stage concerns the social identity of archaic societies and is determined by their mythical worldviews. In these myths nature is anthropomorphized and human social life is naturalized. The result is that no clear distinction is made between such different entities as stones, plants, animals, human beings, and gods. Hence Habermas is "tempted" to compare the social identity of such societies with the "natural identity" of children.

The social identity of members of early civilizations differs from that of archaic societies insofar as their religions differ from the earlier myths. There is an incipient desacralization of the natural environment and a partial autonomy of the political insititutions in respect to the cosmological order. New forms of religious action, such as prayer, sacrifice, and veneration, allow for the development of more defined roles for the individual in relation to the divine being(s). Nevertheless religion has validity only for the particular tribe, people, or community so that the social identity of the group is confined to that community and its specific religion.

With the rise of major world religions, however, this limitation on the development of group identity is overcome. In highly developed civilizations members live with the possibility of "building an ego identity that is detached from all concrete roles and norms" (SI, 92). At the same time the strains upon the world religion in the application of its universal divine commands are also great. For the class divisions and extreme inequalities of power and wealth make it difficult to legitimate the particular state within which the world religion is practiced and at the same time give credence to its universal mission and its universal morality.

Ideologies arise in order to function as "the counterweight to the structural dissimilarity between collective identity tied to the concrete state and ego identities formed within the framework of the universalistic associations" (SI, 93). They also signal the entrance into the fourth stage of the developmental model—namely, the modern era. This is a development in which, according to Habermas, "what is left of universal religions is but the core of universalistic moral systems, and this in greater proportion, the more transparent the infrastructure of monotheistic belief systems has become" (SI, 94). In other words and recalling the previous discussion on the final transition to ego identity, the universal religions have stimulated the development of a higher stage of formal moral reasoning, a stage of universal moral reasoning, which stands in tension with the particular group or collective identities that have in fact arisen historically. The modern social identity will have to be for Habermas a universal identity that removes the split between the formal-developmental level and the social reality.

In addition to this four-stage model of social identity, Hegel is also a major emphasis in the essay, inasmuch as he sees clearly the division (*Entzweiung*) between the individual and society in the modern era and brings it into connection with the alienation of the subject from outer nature and from its inner nature. However, Hegel's solution, contained within the doctrine of absolute spirit, is unsatisfactory to Habermas for several reasons. One reason, that was already noted in the discussion of *Bildung* in chapter 2, lies in the sublation of the processes of externalization and appropriation, on the one hand, and of alienation and reconciliation, on the other. The other and more interesting reason in this context lies in Hegel's identification of the objective spirit of the modern state with the universal aims of absolute spirit. Hegel's identification of the modern state with a rational, universal collective identity is deficient according to Habermas for four reasons. (1) Because Marx's critique of Hegel's philosophy of the state is indeed valid, the bourgeois constitutional state is not a "real" (in the emphatic sense of Hegel's logic) state of universal citizens, but a "merely existing" state of class domination. (2) The sovereignty of modern states is indeed limited by, among other factors, the arms race, the international economy, and the moral factor of world opinion. (3) The complexity of the modern state presents it with steering problems that are beyond its ability to integrate politically and morally. (4) Other political substitutes for the state such as the nation or the party have similarly proven their deficiencies (SI, 96–99).

For Habermas the task remains with Hegel the formation of a *rational* identity (the title of the essay: "Can Complex Societies Form a Rational Identity?"), but Hegel's own solution is unacceptable. More important for our concern is that the contents of traditional worldviews are unacceptable as well. Rather the status of the problem of the formation of a rational social identity and the solution to the problem are to be described as thus:

> As long as we seek for a substitute for a religious doctrine which integrates the normative consciousness of an entire population, we suggest that modern societies likewise constitute their unity still in the form of world views, which put into place (*festschreiben*) a common identity with respect to content. From this we can no longer proceed. Today we can see a collective identity at most in the formal condi- tions under which projections of identity are produced and changed. The individual no longer stands over and against his or her collective identity as a content of tradition on which personal identity can be built as on an established objectivity. Rather individuals themselves must take part in the learning- and will-formation process (*Bildungs- und Willensbildungsprozess*) of a common, first-to-be projected identity. The rationality of the contents of identity is to be measured then alone on the structure of this productive process, i.e. on the formal conditions of the occurrence and the testing of a flexible identity in which all members of society recognize (*wiedererkennen*) themselves and recip- rocally recognize (*anerkennen*), i.e. can respect, one another. For the actual determinant contents philosophy and science, but not only they, can assume a stimulus function (*Anregungsfunktion*), but not a doctrinal function (*Beglaubigungsfunktion*). [ZRHM, 107–8]

Habermas's decided deemphasis of the role of the contents of traditional religions and worldviews in the development of modern social identity marks an equally decided difference in the way that the metaphor of separation and union in the attainment of ego identity must now be understood. Moreover the emphasis placed upon the formal structure of the process of development of both social and ego identity has important consequences for how the *Bildungsprozess* is now conceived. It will be necessary to elaborate on both of these points.

Concerning the model of separation and union, it might be useful to see it first as applied to the relationship of the individual to the group identity of premodern eras. If the correlation between the levels in the development of ego identity and group identity is maintained, then it would appear that a balance is achieved between the individual's role identity and the group identity of either an early or a highly developed civilization. In either instance the individual builds his or her role identity from the collective identity that as a content of tradition functions as an "established objectivity" in Habermas's terms or as "substance" according to Gadamer. In the case of the more highly developed civilizations, there is the further possiblity of the stimulation of an ego identity that is in some sense detached from its personal roles. And thus in this instance there will be a clear sense of separation of the individual from his or her social role. But this separation will be related to a prior union with the contents of tradition, and the balance between separation and union will always be maintained through the dependency of the individual upon a social identity that is already given.

In the modern stage of collective identity formation, if I understand the long quotation correctly, the model of separation and union is applied quite differently. Traditional world religions now serve to form social identity not through their contents, but rather as constructive resources alone. They stimulate in the individual the development of a new level of formal moral reasoning capacity, universalistic moral reasoning, that is at the same time the highest capacity level of the interactive competence. At this highest level of social interaction, the structure or the formal conditions of rationality become reflexive and are used as the means by which a new flexible and universal social identity is to be attained. Habermas writes of the formation of such a flexible social identity that it is a continuous learning process: "Collective identity, and this is the thesis I intend to advance, can today only be grounded in the consciousness of universal and equal chances to participate in the kind of communication processes by which identity formation becomes a continuous learning process" (SI, 99).

As opposed to earlier forms of social identity, the new social identity cannot be articulated through the contents of a worldview. Contents will indeed be necessary; however, rather than fixed contents these contents will always be capable of continuous revision. Similarly, the "new identity can also no longer be that of association or memberships" (SI, 99), for a determination of this kind will be to a particular group rather than to a universal community. Thus instead of the objective spirit of Hegel's modern state or of Gadamer's tradition, the new identity can only be projected into the future, as the "new identity of an as yet emergent global society" (SI, 100). Thus the ego is to balance its personal identity with such a future social identity. Therefore if there is to be union as well as separation, it cannot rest in any past unity but only in the future interpretive accomplishments of individual subjects who have attained the highest level of social interaction.

However, in order for individuals to achieve such universalistic ego structures, the universalistic social identity described by Habermas must be "itself no 'mere projection,' no merely theoretically necessary complement to his notions of individual identity and moral consciousness" (HCE, 40). As Stephen White has observed: "Yet even if Habermas is successful in identifying processes which are undermining traditional sources of collective identity, and thus is able to argue that the question of a new form of identity thereby forces itself onto the agenda, it still has to be viable. . . . Habermas himself finally admits a good deal of uncertainty on this point: 'whether societies in a normal state could develop such a fluid identity is questionable' " (HCE, 40–41).

Habermas's own reservations about the possiblity of a universalistic, continuously fluid social identity aside, it otherwise appears that his account of the process of ego development at this stage in his thought displays most of the same differences with Gadamer that his earlier account of *Bildungsprozess* had in comparison to Gadamer's account of *Bildung*. The major change in his account is the prominent role now given to universal formal competences and to the progressive schemas of a developmental logic. In both instances the effects of rationally reconstuctive sciences and of their distinctions between competence and performance, and above all between content and formal ability, are clearly in evidence. Tradition is not seen primarily as a barrier to self-reflection; however its role is still not a substantive one, but as a stimulus or a "constructive resource" for the development of higher learning abilities. And for the highest level of interactive competence, union is not to be achieved with a past tradition but with a projected future universal community.

Identity and Individuation in *The Theory of Communicative Action*

The Theory of Communicative Action marks a definite watershed in the development of Habermas's thought. If the progression from Hegel through Freud to Piaget that was noted earlier is further pursued, it might now be said to lead to Habermas's own theory of communicative action. The most fundamental level of the earlier three-tiered research program, the general theory of communication, finds its full and complete expression through a critical exposition of and confrontation with the great classic social theorists: Karl Marx and Max Weber, Georg Lukács and the earlier Frankfurt School, George Herbert Mead and Emile Durkheim, Talcott Parsons. In this way, the linguistic turn is also completely effected from a philosophy of consciousness, still at least somewhat in evidence in *Knowledge and Human Interests*, to a theory of communicative action that is a foundation for both an intersubjective theory of socialization and for the theory of social evolution.

The theory of socialization is addressed primarily in the first section of volume 2, which, as McCarthy notes (TCA1, xx), involves a splendid exposition and reconstruction of Mead's social theory. Concerning the subject of primary interest in this chapter, the development of ego identity plays a relatively less major role in the exposition and is actually taken up primarily in an excursus on identity and individuation. This excursus contains an important refinement and distinction in comparison to the earlier writings on ego development. It is also immediately followed by an even more important qualification concerning the entire process of ego development that has important ramifications for all of both Habermas's earlier and present writings on the subject.

The refinement of his earlier views on ego development involves the new distinction between two aspects of ego identity with their own dynamics of development: self-determination and self-realization. In contrast to the earlier emphasis upon solely the universal aspect of ego development, Habermas now writes of two complementary aspects, one universalizing and one particularizing:

> On the one hand, these persons raised under idealized
> conditions learn to orient themselves within a universalistic
> framework, that is, to act autonomously. On the other
> hand, they learn to use this autonomy, which makes them
> equal to every other morally acting subject, to develop
> themselves in their subjectivity and singularity. [TCA2, 97]

The new aspect, the self-realization aspect, is not to be viewed in isolation from the self-determination aspect, but realizes itself on the basis of the acquired autonomy. It involves above all a becoming clear about who one wants to be:

To the extent that the adult can take over and be responsible for his own biography, he can come back to himself in the narratively preserved traces of his own interactions. Only one who takes over his own life history can see in it the realization of his self. Responsibly to take over one's own biography means to get clear about *who one wants to be*, and from this horizon to view the traces of one's own interactions as *if* they were deposited by the actions of a responsible author, of a subject that acted on the basis of a reflective relation to self. [TCA2, 98–99]

The introduction of this new aspect to the treatment of the development of ego identity appears at least initially to present no major modification to Habermas's earlier theory. The development of the capability for self-realization occurs, as would be expected, in the transition of the ego from having a role identity to realizing an ego identity. Moreover it still carries with it the change of orientation from the past toward the future that is the hallmark of Habermas's earlier theory: "At the level of ego-identity a person understands himself in a different way, namely, by answering the question, who or what kind of person he *wants* to be. In place of the orientation to the past, we have an orientation to the future, which makes it possible for the past to become a problem" (TCA2, 106).

At the same time, however, the process of self-realization is made subject to an important qualification, a qualification, I shall wish to argue, that has important ramifications for other parts of his socialization theory, especially for the developmental-logical theory of social identity. In the section immediately following the excursus, Habermas writes:

Ego-identity proves itself in the ability to integrate a series of concrete—partly disintegrated, partly superseded—identities into a life history taken upon oneself; concrete identities, displaced into the past, are in a certain sense *aufgehoben* [cancelled and preserved in a new synthesis] in the individual conduct of life. An autonomous conduct of life depends in turn on the decision—or on successively repeated and revised decisions—as to "who one wants to be." Hitherto I have adopted this existential mode of expression without comment. But this way of describing the situation stylizes what actually takes place in the form of a complex obscure process into a conscious, spontaneously exercised choice. In any case, the answer to the question, who does one want to be, cannot be rational in the way that a moral decision can. . . . There is an indissoluble

element of arbitrariness (*Willkür*) in the choice of a life
project. This is to be explained by the fact that the individual cannot adopt a hypothetical attitude toward his own
origins and background, that he cannot accept or reject his
biography in the same way as he can a norm whose claim
to validity is under discussion. [TCA2, 109]

Habermas's explanation for the impossibility of adopting a
hypothetical attitude toward one's past revolves around the fact that
"the life conduct of an individual is entwined with the life-form of the
collectivity to which he belongs" (TCA2, 110). The decision whether
the life conduct is a good one is not to be decided in the same manner
as in deciding the universality of a moral principle. Rather reference
must be made to the values of the collective life form and ultimately
to its standards of happiness or ideal of the good life. Instead of a
moral question, this is an evaluative question accessible to rational
discussion "only *within the* horizon of a historically concrete form of
life or an individual conduct of life" (MH, 190). Hence the hypothetical attitude of the universal moral reasoner is indeed both impossible
and inappropriate.

Habermas's clear distinction between moral questions and
evaluative questions may itself occasion critical comment, but it is also
important to note that moral questions of principle and evaluative
questions of value do not start off being separate. Rather moral
validity (*Gültigkeit*) and social value (*Geltung*) start off being fused
within the context of the life world (MH, 118). Thus when the moral
agent first assumes the hypothetical attitude of a universal moral
reasoner the "actuality of his or her life world context of experience is
dispersed (*verblasst*)" (MH, 116). The hypothetical mode of procedure
causes a "moralizing" of institutionally ordered relationships in the
same way that cognitive reasoning causes a "theoretizing" of the
external world (MH, 117). Thus the gain in rationality in moral
reasoning carries with it its own "price" in terms of what I interpret to
be an alienating effect, a price that must indeed be "made good on"
(*wettmachen*) by the subsequent application of the abstract moral principle to the concrete practical circumstance (MH, 190).

Habermas's new emphasis upon concrete cultural values represents on his part an attempt, of which he is quite consciously aware, to
incorporate more elements of Hegelian *Sittlichkeit* into the otherwise
strongly Kantian account of *Moralität*. However, I also believe it to be
the case that Gadamerian *Substanz* is being caught up in the assimilation as well. Habermas is aware not only that cultural values are
different from universal norms, but also that ideals of the good life

"stamp the identity of groups and individuals in such a way that they form an integrated part of the respective culture and personality" (MH, 118; in HAS, 19). Moreover, "cultural values also transcend the factual courses of actions (*Handlungsabläufe*); they become concentrated in the historical and biographical syndromes of world orientations, in whose light subjects can distinguish the 'good life' from the reproduction of their 'mere life' (*nackten Lebens*)" (MH, 189).

Cultural values understood in this way appear to influence the formation of collective identity even more than moral principles do. They also appear to be the subject of traditional worldviews and world religions. But in this instance, as perhaps in contrast to the case of moral principles, it must also be the case that the *contents* of tradition are affecting the development of social identity, rather than its moral and cognitive formal structure. In other words, tradition is not working only to stimulate the development of a higher level of evaluation, but rather to establish these values as the values of the historical tradition one belongs to and the social group of which one is a member. And the union that is envisaged is not with any projected world community in the future but with the familiar and local community of the past.

In a passage from a later section of *The Theory of Communicative Action*, Habermas writes, "Action, or mastery of situations presents itself as a circular process in which the actor is at once both the *initiator* of his accountable actions and the *product* of the traditions in which he stands, of the solidary groups to which he belongs, of socialization and learning processes to which he is exposed" (TCA2, 135). No other sentence from the corpus of his work (of for that matter from the corpus of Gadamer's work) better expresses the general thesis or philosophical position toward historical belongingness and personal achievement that is advocated here. The problem from the point of view of Habermas's own theory of socialization is to come up with a sufficient sense of the role of tradition, solidarity, and socialization so that the actor can in fact be said to be their product in addition to being an initiator.

The catalyst role ascribed to tradition in Habermas's earlier theory of the development of social identity is clearly insufficient to accomplish this task. Moreover any approach that would distinguish so clearly between content and formal structure, and relegate the influences of tradition to only the latter aspect, would appear to fail as well. Only when a union with the past is admitted that extends to the contents of its ideals of the good life and to its conception of human happiness, is it also possible to refer to the group identity and the ego identity that results from balancing the group identity with personal identity as being products of this tradition.

The union with the past in this sense also makes it impossible to assume to its fullest extent, of course, a hypothetical attitude or an existentialist posture toward the past in general and not just toward one's own past as Habermas has already observed in *The Theory of Communicative Action*. Indeed he is probably in agreement with this claim and working to incorporate its entailments in a present formulation of his socialization theory. In my estimation, one source that is most useful in elucidating the view of human beings as both products of and initiators within tradition is the writings of Erik Erikson on the themes of identity formation and identity crisis. These writings can be read in support of the impossibility of a totally hypothetical attitude toward past tradition and past socialization, but also—and perhaps even more interestingly—in support of the clinical undesirability of such an attitude as well.

Identity, Fidelity, and Identity Crisis

I wish to present some of the many important themes of Erik Erikson on the topics of identity and identity crisis, but not simply for the purpose of a comparison with the views of Jürgen Habermas. While indeed several clear and perhaps even dramatic contrasts will be drawn to the writings of Habermas on ego development before *The Theory of Communicative Action*—especially in regard to the essay "Can Complex Societies Form a Rational Identity?"—Habermas's views on the development of ego identity have changed in a mitigatory fashion. If my observations above are correct, his earlier views on social identity also have to change; but what is more pertinent, they probably already are in the process of being changed in ways that are consonant with his other modifications.[4]

I primarily wish to utilize Erikson's insights in a manner that is indicated by another of the consequences of Habermas's present effort to integrate Hegelian *Sittlichkeit* with *Moralität*. When he denies that the values of concrete forms of life can be subject to the same standards as morality, he is faced with the question of what sort of standards they are. In answering this question, he states: "Whether the life-form of a collectivity has turned out more or less 'well,' has more or less 'succeeded,' may be a general question we can direct at every form of life, but it is more like a clinical request to judge a patient's mental or spiritual condition than a moral question concerning a norm's or institutional system's worthiness to be recognized" (TCA2, 109). As Peter Dews has commented, "While firmly opposing any politically motivated romanticization of the past, which conveniently neglects the levels of material misery prevalent in premodern societies, Habermas nevertheless insists that our assessment of a form of life as successful or unsuccessful, good or bad, ultimately depends on unformalizable 'clinical' intuitions: a medieval society—even with higher levels of oppression—might be considered less alienated than a modern capitalist metropolis" (HAS, 21). Insofar as there is in this respect the parallel between the life form of a collective and the life history of an individual, the "success" or "unsuccess," "alienation" or "unalienation," of an individual life history is similarly subject to such "clinical" intuitions. And my contention is that some of the most relevant and important clinical intuitions concerning alienation in individual self-formation have been provided by an actual clinician in the attempt to articulate his clinical experiences.

In his most important work, *Childhood and Society*, Erik Erikson gives a condensed formula of his clinical intuitions that were developed in particular by his clinical experiences in the United States. According to this formula, the very aspect of self-realization that is newly distinguished by Habermas from self-determination is, together with the problem of what to believe in, the source of the greatest clinical problems:

> The patient of today suffers most under the problem of
> what he should believe in and who he should—or, indeed,
> might—be or become; while the patient of early psychoa-
> nalysis suffered most under inhibitions which prevented
> him from being what and who he thought he knew he was.
> In this country especially, adult patients and the parents of
> prospective child patients often hope to find in the psycho-
> analytic system a refuge from the discontinuities of exis-
> tence, a regression and a return to a more patriarchal one-
> to-one relationship. [C&S, 279]

Erikson designated the sufferings of his patients "character disorders" in order to distinguish them from neuroses and psychoses and their classic case histories. Rather than addressing himself to the internal mechanisms of repression and defense, he found himself confronting primarily problems of social interaction: "What in Freud's day, then, was a neurotic epidemiology with social implications has, in our times, become a series of social movements with neurotic implications" (IY&C, 29). Thus when Erikson refers to the "discontinuities of existence" in the above passage, he is alluding above all to the discontinuities of social existence and the deleterious effects of these discontinuities upon his younger and older patients. Concerning these effects, Erikson opposes a return to an earlier form of social relationship on both a personal and societal level, but he also is acutely aware of the potentially "neurotic implications" of even progressive social discontinuity. Thus it is his "clinical judgments" about both the positive and negative aspects of social discontinuity, above all in the transition from childhood to adulthood, that are of primary interest in the comparison with Habermas.

Freud formulated his classic case histories in terms of his very important theory and developmental pattern of psychosexual development. Erikson interprets character disorders under the backdrop of the development of personal identity and thus raises it to a central position within psychoanalytic theory. Concerning personal identity, he writes: "we deal with a process 'located' *in the core of the individual* and yet also *in the core of his communal culture*, a process which establishes in fact, the identity of those two identities" (IY&C, 22). But this concern for personal identity also entails for Erikson the modification of classic Freudian theory: "The traditional psychoanalytic method, on the other hand, cannot grasp identity because it has not developed terms to conceptualize the environment" (IY&C, 24).[5] Hence Erikson proposes the inclusion of an epigenetic scheme of psychosocial development of the ego to complement Freud's theory of psychosexual development of the libido.

In addition to Freud's classic account of how the undifferentiated forces of the libido undergo a process of differentiation and development through the oral, anal, and phallic stages to the final genital stage of sexual development, Erikson proposes two further stages—puberty and adulthood—to make it more fully correlative to his own account of psychosocial development. Within this developmental pattern, the individual modes or "preformed action pattern" of drive expression are related to the social modalities or different interpersonal ways of interacting with these modes in order to produce a comprehensive account of the psychosocial development of the ego. The result is a famous eight-stage model of ego development, within which each stage presents a particular conflict or crisis, which must be overcome before the next stage can be entered. Chart 1 shows these stages, together with the corresponding biological ages, and also the corresponding stages in the psychosexual pattern of development (IY&C, 166).

In the specific stage of ego identity in the chart of the life cycle, the point of departure for all of Erikson's clinical and theoretical

Chart 1

Stages of Ego Development, with Corresponding
Biological and Psychosexual Stages

AGE	PSYCHOSOCIAL CRISIS	PSYCHOSEXUAL STAGE
Infancy	Trust vs. Mistrust	Oral
Early Childhood	Autonomy vs. Shame	Anal
Play Age	Initiative vs. Guilt	Infantile-Genital
School Age	Industry vs. Inferiority	"Latency"
Adolescence	Identity vs. Identity Confusion	Puberty
Young Adulthood	Intimacy vs. Isolation	Genitality
Adulthood	Generosity vs. Self-Absorption	
Old Age	Integrity vs. Despair	

innovations becomes focalized, as the very name of the stage—identity formation—indicates. Although considerations of identity formation may become evident in the immediately preceding stage and certainly are important for assessing the following stages, Erikson contends that it is this specific stage within which many of the clinical problems for contemporary psychotherapy arise. Moreover it was for this stage that Erikson coined the term that has gained him the greatest fame, "identity crisis." I will wish to discuss some of the themes concerning identity and identity crisis, and compare them with the more formal and developmental-logical treatment of identity development in the pre-*Theory of Communicative Action* writings of Habermas.

Adolescence, or the period in which identity is usually acquired, is characterized by Erikson in terms of a psychosocial moratorium. This is "a period of sexual and cognitive maturation and yet a sanctioned postponement of definitive commitment" (LCC, 75). It is a period of transitional status between being a child and being an adult, and, as such, it is observed to be a feature of almost all societies. However, in our culture it has a particularly protracted status with a longer and longer period being alloted to schooling, social training, and role experimentation.[6]

Youth in our society are confronted with many tasks and challenges within their psychosocial moratoria: the development of the capability to be physically intimate, the need to make a decisive occupational choice, the exposure to competition with peers, and the demands for psychosocial self-definition (I&LC, 133). Concerning contemporary society, Erikson also believes:

along with structural differentiation and professional
specialization, children become more isolated from society
as a whole, less a part of the meaningful occupational
pursuits of their fathers, more a separate subculture unto
themselves. This means that the bridging rituals—the
rituals between adults and children designed to recognize
and to educate the child as well as to confirm and to renew
the adult—are weakened, if not altogether destroyed. With
these rituals of transmission and inclusion weakened, the
child and the adolescent have a greater task of synthesis to
accomplish, often under greater pressure and with fewer
supports. The generational distance is further aggravated
by a frantic rate of technologically induced social change
and general social and financial mobility. [GM, 170]

Because of the change of the nature of the transitional status
in modern societies and because of the social isolation that is now
involved in the psychosocial moratorium, Erikson refers to a general
sense of "uprootedness" in modernity. Uprootedness correlates
closely to estrangement or division (*Entzweiung*) in Hegel as the
following quotation from Donald Browning makes clear: "Uprootedness tends to deprive modern man, and especially the children of
modern man, of . . . that sense of activating 'recognition' which
confirms one's uniqueness while it gives definition and support to
one's possibilities" (GM, 171). Because of uprootedness, the lack of
commitment characteristic of all forms of psychological moratoria is
or at least may be subjectively experienced in the modern psychological moratorium as a crisis of identity. Thus Erikson is (perhaps
consciously)[7] integrating the Hegelian sense of alienation into the
clinical judgments he makes about the modern acquisition of identity.

Erikson also advocates a balance between personal and social
identity in his account of identity formation in much the same way
that Habermas expressed in an early stage of his writing, and was
noted in chapter 3. One aspect of the specific stage of identity formation is the aspect "by which the individual judges himself in the light
of what he perceives to be the way in which others judge him in
comparison to themselves and to a typology significant to them"
(IY&C, 22). In addition to this aspect, there is the further aspect that
the individual "judges their way of judging him in the light of how he
perceives himself in comparison to them and to types that have
become relevant to him" (IY&C, 22–23).

Finally Erikson writes of ego identity: "The growing child must
derive a vitalizing sense of reality from the awareness that his individual way of mastering experience (his ego synthesis) is a successful

variant of a group identity and is in accord with its space-time and life plan" (C&S, 235). In speaking of an individual identity that is a "successful variant" of group identity, he is giving expression to the balancing to be maintained between personal identity and social identity, a task that falls to the ego identity that is being formed.

Erikson also appeals to Piaget, but with a different application of his thought in mind that relates more directly to the formation of ego identity. Erikson agrees with Habermas in his interpretation of Piaget that "the adolescent, before beginning to manipulate the material at hand, as the pre-adolescent would do with little hesitation, waits and hypothesizes on the possible results, even as he lingers after the experiment and tries to fathom the truth behind the known results" (I&R, 171). However, Erikson relates the attainment of this cognitive ability not to the attainment of a higher level of moral reasoning ability, but to the formulation of what he calls "the historical perspective": "This capacity forms, I think, a basis for the development, in later adolescence, of the *historical perspective*, which makes room not only for imaginative speculation about all that could have happened in the past, but also a deepening concern with the narrowing down of vast possibilities to a few alternatives, often resolved only by a 'totalistic' search for single causes" (I&R, 171).

Youth is "preoccupied with the danger of hopeless determination, be it by irreversible childhood identifications, by ineradicable secret sins or socially 'stacked' conditions" (I&R, 171). Thus, "what we consider an interpretation to youth easily becomes a statement of doom" (I&R, 171). The attainment of a "historical perspective" can allow the adolescent to distinguish what is truly irreversible or ineradicable from what are as yet free and undetermined opportunities of choice. Therefore the application of Piaget plays a crucial role in the resolution of an identity crisis for Erikson, whereas Habermas's application leads to the establishment of a universal standard of moral reasoning.

Concerning the dangers that can arise in respect to the formation and maintenance of ego identity in the age of adolescence, Erikson has written:

> We have described the prime danger of this age, therefore, as identity confusion, which can express itself in excessively prolonged moratoria . . . or in repeated impulsive attempts to end the moratorium with sudden choices—that is, to play with historical possibilities—and then deny that some irreversible commitment has already taken place, or sometimes also in severe regressive pathology. [IY&C, 246]

To prolong the moratorium, to avoid making choices or a commitment, promotes both the social sense of isolation and the inner sense of being "not-quite-somebody." On the other hand, "decisions and choices and, most of all, successes in any direction bring to the fore conflicting identifications and immediately threaten to narrow down the inventory of further tentative choices; and, at the very moment when time is of the essence, every move may establish a binding precedent in psychosocial self-definition" (I&LC, 133). Thus the dangers to the maintenance of the balance are, similar to Habermas's earlier writings on identity, either being totally isolated from or totally bound by one's psychosocial definition.

Erikson believes that the experiencing of identity confusion and identity crisis is indeed conducive to important personal growth; however, his "clinical judgments" concerning the attainment of that growth are couched in considerably less optimistic terms than in the description of adolescence in "Can Complex Societies Form a Rational Identity?" For example, he is, like Habermas, an advocate of universal ethics—although with one significant difference. For Erikson the attainment of this desirable progression from tribal morality or pseudo species identification with one's own group in opposition to other groups is to be situated in adulthood—if it is to occur at all—and not in adolescence. Erikson correlates a moral stage with childhood and a universal ethical stage with adulthood, but he interposes an *ideological* stage between the two.

Concerning the term "ideology" Erikson explains:

> The need to bind irrational self-hate and irrational repudiation makes young people, on occasion, morally compulsive and conservative even where and when they seem most anarchic and radical; the same need makes them potentially "ideological," i.e., more or less explictly in search of a world image held together by what [George Bernard] Shaw called "a clear comprehension of life in the light of an intelligible theory." ... More generally, an ideological system is a coherent body of shared images, ideas, and ideals which (whether based on a formulated dogma, an implicit *Weltanschauung*, a highly structured world image, a political creed, or a "way of life") provides for the participants a coherent, if systematically simplified, over-all orientation in space and time, in means and ends. [I&LC, 169]

Ideological systems deal with values—not primarily as Habermas has distinguished them from moral principles through reference to the ideals of the good life, but as the values of one's group, one's community, one's country, one's tradition. The virtue that Erikson correlates with the successful resolution of identity crisis in adolescence is fidelity. It is defined by Erikson as "the ability to sustain loyalties freely pledged in spite of the inevitable contradictions of value systems" (I&R, 125).

For Erikson the search for an ideology to be faithful to and the achievement of ego identity are considered to be "two aspects of the same process" (I&LC, 168) in adolescence.[8] With the putting forward of this claim, he is advocating a balance of separation and union now not between personal and social identity, but rather, as articulated in the previous chapter, between personal initiative and social structure and tradition. Erikson writes of the stage of ego identity: "The dominant issue of this as of any other stage, therefore, is the assurance that the active, the selective ego is in charge and enabled to be in charge by a social structure which grants a given age group the place it needs—and in which it is needed" (IY&C, 246). Encapsulated in this statement is a balance between, on the one hand, being a product of one's tradition and being assigned one's place by one's social structure and, on the other hand, being a personal initiator within one's tradition and achieving within one's social structure. If I interpret it correctly, the balance is endangered by cultural uprootedness and social isolation, on the one hand, and traditional authoritarianism and social conformity on the other. Or, if yet another formulation may be attempted, it is finally a balance between the basic belongingness in one's biological, social, and traditional "rootedness" and the rational trust to be achieved through the social cooperation inherent in communicative action.

With the emphasis upon both identity formation and fidelity, Erikson is stating that modern youth, as the youth of all previous eras and as modern adults as well, need both to achieve their own personal identity and yet maintain a sense of continuity with the ideals and aspirations of their own tradition. The subjectively experienced identity crises can be attributed to at least as much, if not more than, a lack of connectedness with one's culture as a lack of personal initiative, as Jerome Bruner explains in regard to Erikson's treatment of the Black Panther movement:

> A healthy identity is not simply a state of the psyche in
> isolation, but a connection one has with one's culture, a
> connection that encourages aspiration and provides means
> for effective action even if in opposition. For Erikson Huey
> Newton and the Panthers were not on a neurotic trip.
> They were battling for connection, for a place and means
> for growth—even if in enraged opposition. [AA, 10]

If Erikson makes a quite negative and harsh judgment in this example, it is not about the psychological state of a group of young revolutionaries, but rather about their social surroundings that make it so difficult for them to "search for something and someone to be true to" (IY&C, 235) in their present circumstances. It is up to the social structure to grant the Black Panther movement the "place it needs," even if the place is to be used ultimately "in enraged opposition" to the social structure.

My belief is that Erikson has made "clinical judgments" not only about the psychological condition of his patients and about the ideals of the good life in our society, but also about the balance between being situated within the biological, social, and historical processes of development and being actors within that same process. Because a sense of connectedness with culture and tradition is not a subsidiary accomplishment in comparison to the development of healthy identity, it is not supplantable by the projection of a future social identity based upon an anticipated world society. Thus there is an aspect of hermeneutical situatedness "at work" in Erikson's description of the formation of ego identity that is not always similarly present in Habermas's rational reconstruction of the same process.

It is for this reason that I believe that the Eriksonian eight-stage description of the life cycle not only has deficiencies in terms of a universal theory of rational reconstruction but also great offsetting virtues in respect to its content. Erikson's description of the different stages of the life cycle can be considered formally defective as a universal developmental theory because of the number of stages and the lack of clearly defined and ordered formal rational operations in differentiating them. Moreover the very description of the conflicts in the later stages of the theory may raise the suspicion that Erikson's theory is closely connected to a Western concept of the family and to historical developments of modernity.[9] Nevertheless this same cause for suspicion from a formal standpoint also gains for Erikson's description of the later stages of the life cycle a hermeneutical relevance that is essential for comprehending the historical dimensions, including the contents of tradition, that have contributed to the development of—and produced—the personal and social identities that we as a matter of fact have. Therefore Erikson's description of the life cycle is an exemplar of what I believe to be *hermeneutically informed* and *hermeneutically situated social science*. The metaphor of balance, in both the original Habermasian sense and according to my modification, is better preserved in Erikson's account precisely because of its hermeneutical situatedness, and his concern for historical connectedness hermeneutically informs the way identity formation is described.

At the same time, however, as this aspect of hermeneutical situatedness and hermeneutical informedness is evident in Erikson's description of ego identity, it is not necessarily understood in the same way as Hans-Georg Gadamer conceives it—as the manner in which Erikson seeks to account for identity formation indicates. Erikson may judge that a state of "identity crisis" is attributable to modern youth because of a lack of connectedness to the past. Nevertheless this past is not simply belonged to "beyond our willing and doing" but one which also, in Bruner's words, "encourages aspiration" and "provides means for effective action." There is an aspect of personal achievement that balances with the sense of historical belongingness and is necessary for the identity crisis to be overcome. In the next chapter, Erikson's characterization of the "social play" of adolescents and the way in which it enables a successful transition to adulthood will be examined, after his analysis of childhood play is compared and contrasted with Gadamer's description of play already discussed in chapter 1.

5

The Action
Structure of Childhood and
Adolescent Play

I n the last chapter I asserted that Erikson's description of the life
cycle is an exemplar of hermeneutically situated and hermeneutically informed social science. This chapter, I hope, will allow this
claim to gain in plausibility and credibility. The main reason I
believe that a hermeneutical standpoint informs the description of
the life cycle is that some of the same phenomena at the heart of
Gadamer's thought are being dealt with and attributed the same
central role in Erikson's thinking: play and *Bildung* as a process of
education and self-formation. Where Erikson differs from Gadamer
in the description of these phenomena is not in a denial of any important aspect of historical situatedness—hence the claim of hermeneutically situated social science—but rather in the emphasis placed upon
individual mastery as essential to childhood play and to what Erikson
terms the "social play" of adolescents. Therefore I will compare
Gadamer's descriptions of play and *Bildung* with Erikson's descriptions of childhood play and social play in order to explicate an "action
structure" I find characteristic of the latter descriptions. This action
structure will be compared to the happening structure of Gadamer
and a complementarity of both structures will be urged in repect to
the same processes of appropriation, education, and self-formation.
It is this complementarity, if accepted, that can lead to a more positive assessment of personal achievement without the denial of historical belongingness.

In the first section of this chapter, I will compare Gadamer's description of play and its entailments that were examined in chapter 1 with Erik Erikson's description of the play of a five-year-old boy in his book, *Toys and Reasons*.[1] If there is a literary-phenomenological Erikson, the place where he is most a literary critic and most a phenomenologist is in chapter 6 of *Childhood and Society*, "Toys and Reasons," and also in his subsequent book of the same title. The title itself is taken from two lines of a poem by William Blake: "The child's toys and the old man's reasons / are the fruits of the two seasons." This verse is used by Erikson as the point of departure for his descriptions and analyses of childhood play. At the conclusion of the first section of his chapter, "Toys and Reasons," he comments on the results of his work:

> What is infantile play, then? We saw that it is not the
> equivalent of adult play, that it is not recreation. The
> playing adult steps sideward into another reality; the
> playing child advances forward to new stages of mastery.
> [C&S, 222]

Gadamer's description of play has the very considerable merit of being a description of "more than" recreation and of disclosing a reality that is not simply sidewards to everyday reality but indeed reveals its deepest dimension. However, one reason for making a comparison between him and Erikson on the subject of play is the acute sensitivity that Erikson displays toward the difficulties of describing and respectfully analyzing the play of infants, children, and adolescents. Child's play is definitely not, as the expression goes, "child's play" for him. He writes that "only he who enters the child's world as a polite guest and studies play as a most serious occupation learns what a child thinks when he is not forced to adapt himself to the verbalized and classified world" (EE, 76). A major difficulty is that adults are not apt to be polite guests: because adult play is governed by the attitude that "whoever does not work shall not play," adults have to be motivated even simply to tolerate play. As Erikson explains: "The most popular theory and the easiest on the observer is that the child is *nobody yet*, and that the nonsense of his play reflects it" (C&S, 214).

However, there is a much more important reason than possible adult misconceptions for taking up the toys of the child and relating them to the phenomenological description of play in *Truth and Method*. That reason is the profound differences between Gadamer's description of the event-character of play that catches its participants up into the happening of the play and Erikson's description of childhood play. Continuing the quotation from "Toys and Reasons" cited above, we can compare Erikson's theory of childhood play and his view of adult activity that follows from it:

> I propose the theory that the child's play is the infantile form of the human ability to deal with experience by creating model situations and to master reality by experiment and planning. It is in certain phases of his work that the adult projects past experience into dimensions which seem manageable. In the laboratory, on the stage, and on the drawing board, he relives the past and thus relieves leftover affects; in reconstructing the model situation, he redeems his failures and strengthens his hopes. He anticipates the future from the point of view of a corrected and shared past. [C&S, 222][2]

As will be clarified further in the first section of this chapter, Erikson imputes to the playing child a strong interest in and capability for the mastery of its physical environment and its social experience. Moreover this sense of mastery is evident not only in the toys of childhood but also, as seen in the second section of this chapter, in the social play of adolescents.

What makes individual mastery and the importance of personal achievement so evident in Erikson's descriptions of childhood play and adolescent social play is what I term their "action structure." In the third and final section of this chapter, I develop the basic features of this structure in contrast with Gadamer's analysis of the *Geschehen* character of play. In his description of the protected play of children, Erikson emphasizes how personal achievement is enabled by historical and familial belongingness rather than, in the first instance, how it is limited by history and familial association. In addition, the importance of the aspect of personal achievement is conveyed through references to the actions or accomplishments of children and adolescents in addition to the language of event or occurrence that surrounds them and catches them up. Finally, the importance of being and feeling able to act or be competent is especially seen in the social play of adolescents who are trying within their social play to resolve the identity crises in which they are involved. This more active description of the process of self-formation can be said to provide Erikson with his own implicit account of *Bildung*, which is presented as a complement, not competitor, to Gadamer's more famous treatment of the same process.

Child's Play

Erikson's descriptions of childhood play stem from his clinical observations of the phenomenon. Nevertheless it might be misleading to call him simply an "observer" of the play of children. Of his role in play therapy he explains:

> Modern play therapy is based on the observation that a child made ambivalent and insecure by a secret hate against or fear of the natural protectors of his play (family, neighborhood) seems able to use the protective sanction of an understanding adult, in professional elaboration the play therapist, to regain some play peace. [WLT, 142]

In his interactive role as an understanding adult, as a play therapist or, in general, as a play protector, Erikson has observed a broad variety of games with an equally broad variety of purposes. Concerning these purposes, Robert Coles has commented:

> Games can have their own meaning, and need not be seen as anything but what they are, a way to fill up the child's time, energy and interest. Games are also social occasions, when children can meet to share feeling and display skill. Yet there are times when a game becomes a very personal thing, an expression of what is most on a child's mind. For Erikson *all* these considerations are important. It is not a matter of going from a "superficial" interpretation of play as "mere" activity or as stylized social behavior to a "deep interpretation" of play as an outpouring of unconscious energy symbolically directed. Rather the child's develop-ment, his progressively diverse involvement with people and things, sets the stage for his activities, fun and games included. [EE, 129]

Erikson's earliest example of an infantile game originates with Freud. It is the most famous game in the entire tradition of psychoa-nalysis and at the same time one of the sources of its strongest disputes. The game involves an eighteen-month-old child and a wooden bobbin with a piece of string tied around it. The child would throw the bobbin away ('with considerable skill') and then pull it back. When the bobbin was thrown away, the child expressed a long, drawn out "O-o-o-oh," which was interpreted by its mother and by Freud as an attempt to say *fort*, the German word for "gone" or "away." When the bobbin was pulled back, the child happily said *da* or "here" in

German. Freud observed that the mother often left the child alone for long periods to fend for itself. He interpreted the child's actions as the playful attempt to deal with the mother's alternating disappearence and reappearence by turning *passivity* into *activity*, by attempting to play at doing something with the bobbin that was in reality being done to him by his mother. This desire for mastery has been taken by ego psychoanalysts since Freud as a clear sign of the important role of the independent ego within psychic life. At the same time this appeal to a sense of mastery and the strong theoretical role attributed to the ego have also come under attack from strong opponents of ego psychoanalysis such as Jacques Lacan. Lacan has offered in turn his own ingenious interpretations of the *fort-da* game that make no such reference to a sense of mastery in the playing child.[3]

This study is not directly interested in the polemics surrounding ego psychoanalysis or in the related difficult question of Erikson's relation to ego psychoanalysis.[4] Erikson does interpret the game with the bobbin in accordance with his more general thesis concerning the role of mastery in childhood play. As such, it is one example in a vast panorama of childhood play that is organized following Erikson's developmental sequence. For the early stages of the life cycle, he correlates different forms of play to different types of ritualizations as follows: infancy, mutuality of (face to face) recognition; early childhood, discrimination of good and bad; play age, dramatic elaboration; school age, rules of performance; and adolescence, solidarity of conviction (T&R, 85–113; WLT, 575–94). Thus for the infant, but even more for children at later stages of development, this "new mastery is not restricted to the technical mastery of toys and *things*; it also includes an infantile way of mastering *experiences* by meditating, experimenting, planning and sharing" (I&LC, 90).

Probably Erikson's most powerful description of childhood play as the mastery of experience, rather than the technical mastery over a thing, involves the dramatic play of the "play age" and concerns the block construction of a five-year-old black boy, Robert. He provides his own description of Robert's play in the world of manageable toys (which is termed the microsphere in contrast to the macrosphere of the larger and adult social world) that can be compared with Gadamer's description of play in *Truth and Method*:

> In Robert's construction, the tall structure [see diagram], as
> we claimed, represents a dancing gesture of locomotor self-
> assertion which might help overcome the conflicts and

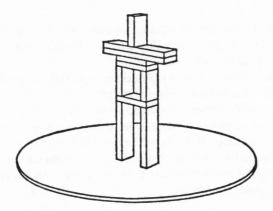

traumata alluded to in the side scenes. In the center is the image of a boy-in-the-making, who will learn new ways of integrating bodily grace and vigor with the capacity to comprehend and to learn. But, as we noted, this boy's uneasiness over the reconciliation of bodily expression and mental discipline extends to much of his cultural setting.... The total event, then, is an experimentation in the microsphere with a new identity element embedded in a new sense of community. Such a basic spatial theme, however, contains some temporal coordinates relating past traumata and solutions to fearful as well as hopeful aspects of the future.... Thus, the recapitulation of a possible doom is turned into a promised renewal through playful mastery in the present: maybe one will grow up whole, and there is a chance of growing up loving and lovable. [T&R, 44–45; diagram is from p. 31][5]

Erikson admits that the formula for his description is only "implicit" in the play of Robert and of other children. He also states that he is using "mythical" words to describe Robert's play but adds "—too mythical for a child's vocabulary, but not, I would think, for his experiential feelings" (T&R, 45). These experiential feelings include for Erikson a sense of dread because of the past and a need to believe in a different future, the need to "feel reassurance of the chance of subduing destructive forces within and fighting off inimical ones without" (T&R, 45) and, finally and most importantly for our context, the need "to feel like a new being capable of utilizing new competencies in a widening present" (T&R, 45).

Erikson writes in general of the "dramatic" play in childhood that it "provides the *infantile form of the human propensity to create model situations in which aspects of the past are re-lived, the present re-presented and renewed, and the future anticipated*" (T&R, 44). His interpretation of the block construction is that it is such an attempt by a five-year-old boy to create a "model situation" of his life. The boy is, like the adult in the quotation from "Toys and Reasons" quoted above, reliving the past in a way that relieves his fears. He is also redeeming in the present his past failures and above all strengthening his hopes for the future by anticipating a time when he may be whole and when he will be both loving and lovable.

Erikson confesses to the employment of "big words for word-less play" (T&R, 45), but such words could be valuable for the phenomenological description of play that takes childhood play just as seriously as adult play. They also make for an interesting comparison with Gadamer's description of play in *Truth and Method*.[6] That description, especially as conveyed in the claim that "all playing is a being played," is the best description in the entire work of the event structure that also characterizes Gadamer's discussion of conversation and language, tradition and history. It is a description of players immersed in the to-and-fro movements of the game to such a degree that they lose themselves in the event that is happening to them. This "way of being" of play is, of course, the same "way of being" of tradition or the way that tradition happens. This description of the way tradition happens allows Dieter Misgeld to write in complete fidelity with Gadamer's views that "tradition is operative on us by forming our personal and social preoccupations before we can pass judgment on them."[7]

Erikson's description of play contrasts with Gadamer's description not by denying an experience of belongingness to play but by asserting an experience of mastery even within the play of a five-year-old boy. The "big words for wordless play" of children convey the presence of a youthful, playful mastery, which involves meditating and experimenting on experience, and planning and sharing it. And this active attempt to master experience within a protective environment, while it need not oppose directly any sense of being played, can be used in support of a very interesting counterpart I can construct to Misgeld's statement about tradition. For if tradition is indeed operative on us before our becoming aware of it, for Erikson "achievement is active in us by helping form our personal and social preoccupations before we can pass judgment on the manner in which we are active." Or, as Erikson himself insists after stating his theory on the role of mastery in childhood play quoted in the Introduction to this chapter, "no thinker can do more and no playing child less" (C&S, 222).

The Social Play of Adolescents on Bali and in Saxon Germany

The period of adolescence falls at the borderline between the periods of childhood and adulthood, and is positioned between the spheres of play and work. As noted above in chapter 4, Erikson considers the adolescent to be involved in a "psychosocial moratorium" between the childhood world of play and the adulthood world of work and politics. This psychosocial moratorium is characterized as involving transitional status, lack of commitment, and isolation from society's mainstream. Of course the last two aspects may be taken to pertain only to the youth of modern Western nations, but the very stage of adolescence for all cultures is described above all by its transitional status. In relation to the period of childhood that precedes it and the state of adulthood that follows it, it is a period, in Erikson's terms, of "social play" rather than childhood play or adult work and recreation.

For many of the same reasons as in the earlier case of the play of children, the social play of adolescents stands in danger of being misunderstood by adults. Of adults in relation to the behavior of adolescents, Erikson writes: "We alternately consider such behavior irrelevant, unnecessary, or irrational, and ascribe to it purely regressive and neurotic meanings" (I&LC, 126–27). Concerning the vicissitudes in the outcomes of such play, he adds:

> Whether or not a given adolescent's newly acquired capacities are drawn back into infantile conflict depends to a significant extent on the quality of the opportunities and rewards available to him in his peer clique, as well as on the more formal ways in which society at large invites a transition from social play to work experimentation, and from rituals of transit to final commitments. [I&LC, 127]

From what Clifford Geertz writes of the Balinese cockfights described in chapter 3, they may well have afforded such formal opportunities "in classical times" (before 1908) for young Balinese males to make the important transition to adulthood. He states that "the staging of a cockfight was an explicitly societal matter" (IC, 424) and that bringing "a cock to an important fight was, for an adult male, a compulsory duty of citizenship" (IC, 424). Yet even if the formal status of the cockfight was lost (due to the interference of foreign rule), the same result may be described as coming about even in a necessarily less formal way. For Geertz also writes, as was quoted earlier, that "attending cockfights and participating in them is, for the Balinese, a kind of sentimental education' (IC, 449). The cockfight for the Balinese is a "paradigmatic human event" according to Geertz, "binding them into a set of rules which at once contains them and allows them play, builds a symbolic structure in which, over and over again, the reality of their inner affiliation can be intelligibly felt" (IC, 450).

Geertz gives no specific analysis of the relationship of the cockfight to the young Balinese observer who aspires to be a cockfighter, but the insights from Erikson on the nature of social play can be employed in support and in furtherance of Geertz's conclusion. Geertz describes the "true" Balinese cockfighter as possessing a very high status in his society. It is a status that is put in risk by the uncertain course of action of the cockfight, yet is more likely to be confirmed by the cock's training for battle regardless of the actual outcome of the fight. Consequently the attainment of this status is a difficult personal accomplishment that is spoken about by Balinese males "in that almost venerative way" (IC, 435). Insights from Erikson on the nature of games and the aspirations of adolescents can be integrated with this description of the venerated, "true" Balinese cockfighter in order to produce an account of the "social play" of the young male who both watches the cockfight spectacle in aspiration of being a "true" Balinese cockfighter and commits himself to that aspiration.

Erikson's best description of socially important adult games must itself be modified to pertain to the example of a battle of trainers and cocks. His description concerns a team game where adult human beings are the principals. Nevertheless the modification is not difficult, if for team is understood alternatively the tandem of the cockfighter and his cock or, at times, the alliance of cockfighter and his band of relatives and supporters. The skill of the human principal is measured in terms of his ability as a trainer, and the name and trappings of the team are carried over to the combatant roosters. Of games in general Erikson writes:

> Institutionalized games take place bounded in a special
> space and a programmed time. A set number of partici-
> pants is divided into opposite but equal teams, each distin-
> guished by insignia and often also a magic name. This
> field may be surrounded by viewers— themselves divided
> in their team sympathies. The game as a test of loyalty,
> skill, and fate is decided in favor of one team, while the
> other is guaranteed another chance. Thus, each side, while

highly committed in its loyalties, remains exchangeably identified with the opponent who is expert in the same sport, accepts the same rules, is subject to the same fate, and thus in principle, takes an equal chance. Furthermore, each player, on either side, must have learned to adapt himself, at least while he plays, to a gamemanship combining passion and restraint, discipline and originality—all of which promises to make the best players charismatic symbols. . . . In such game reality, symbolic acts can be committed, symbolic emotions experienced, and alternations of symbolic doom and triumph accepted which in "real life" might mean the absolute dominance or total defeat of one of the other side. [T&R, 71–72]

Erikson's analysis of games and the role of social play concurs with Geertz that attending and participating in the Balinese cockfight is an important instance of sentimental education, understood even as sentimental *Bildung*. He writes of such games that they "stand midway between individual play in the toy world and the arena of politics in which human beings unite in communal interplay and establish rules for joining and for contesting with one another" (T&R, 72). The social play of the Balinese youth occupies this same midway status, especially when he watches the "true" Balinese cockfighter and considers for himself what the possibility of active participation in the cockfight could mean. Concerning such watching from the point of view of owner and bettor, Geertz writes: "As he watches fight after fight, with the active watching of an owner and a bettor . . . , he grows familiar with it and what it has to say to him, much as the attentive listener to string quartets or the absorbed viewer of still lifes grows slowly more familiar with them in a way which opens his subjectivity to himself" (IC, 450–51). Where Erikson's analysis adds to this description is in what it entails for young aspirants to experience the emotions stirred up by the cockfight and want to "mean" them personally for themselves. As he writes of the young Luther, "for an affect to have a deep and lasting effect . . . , it must not only be experienced as nearly overwhelming, but it must also in some way be affirmed by the ego as valid, almost as chosen: one means the affect, it signifies something meaningful, it is significant" (YML, 209).

For a youthful observer of the cockfight, the decision to participate actively as a cockfighter entails both, in Geertz's description, the chance to play a more prominent role in the sentimental education of oneself and other group members and, according to Erikson's insights, the responsibility of "meaning" this education and making it significant for oneself in an act of self-formation.[8] Geertz's judgment that the "Balinese forms and discovers his temperament and his society's temper at the same time" appears to be apt as a characterization of what is involved for the adolescent Balinese in making the transition to adulthood. Or in Erikson's own words, the cockfight represents a "combination of freedom and discipline, of adventure and tradition" (YML, 42) in respect to the adolescent who, through "social play," sees and imagines what he most wants to be. In aspiring to be and in deciding to become a "true" Balinese cockfighter, he participates in an affective process of *Bildung* both of and, with the decision, also profoundly by himself.

This characterization of Eriksonian social play as a process of *Bildung* is borne out in even stronger detail, if the transition to adulthood is conceived not as continuous, but rather as the result of overcoming a subjectively experienced crisis. In his description of identity crisis in *Young Man Luther*, Erikson describes Luther as involved in the already alluded to problem; namely, "to combine intellectual meaning with an inner sense of meaning it" (YML, 176). This problem manifested itself in the young man through a "tortuous self-consciousness, characterized at one time by shame over what one is already sure one is, and at another time by doubt as to what one may become":

> A person with this self-consciousness often cannot work,
> not because he is not gifted and adept, but because his
> standards preclude any approach that does not lead to
> being outstanding; while at the same time these standards
> do not permit him to compete to defeat others. [YML,
> 101]

Luther becomes confident in his own capability, his identity, and his ability to mean what he thinks by undergoing a process of self-formation that Erikson finds characteristic of other rebellious youth in Western settings. He provides a description of this process of *Bildung* that can be compared with that of Gadamer as described in chapter 2:

> At this point we must note a characteristic of young great
> rebels: their inner split between the temptation to
> surrender and the need to dominate. A great young rebel
> is torn between on the one hand tendencies to give in and
> phantasies of defeat . . . and the absolute need on the
> other hand, to take the lead not only over himself but over

all the forces and people who impinge on him. In men of ideas, the second, the dictatorial trend, may manifest itself paradoxically at first in a seeming surrender to passivity which, in the long run, proves to have been an active attempt at liquidating passivity by becoming fully acquainted with it. . . . Paradoxically, many a young man becomes a great man in his own sphere only be learning that deep passivity which permits him to let the data of his competency speak to him. [YML, 156–57, 207][9]

Eriksonian *Bildung*, if it can be termed as such, stands in this instance in a particularly complementary *and* opposed relation to Gadamer's description of the same process. Gadamer's goal in his description of *Bildung* is to preserve the role of tradition by letting it speak to one with its full power. Erikson writes of a deep passivity as well, but its role is to let one's competency speak to one. Gadamer's description of what might indeed more properly be termed the assimilation of tradition rather that its appropriation is that it is the activity of the *Sache*, the thing, the issue, the subject matter of the conversation or the content of tradition that is at the same time a passivity. Erikson's description of what can probably only be termed young Luther's appropriation of Christianity rather than its assimilation is that it is a passivity of Luther that at the same time is an activity. If it is a passivity in both instances, it is an active passivity; but in the one instance it is a happening of tradition, an event, while in the other instance it is a passivity in the service of regaining a sense of initiative and mastery, and hence, although passive, ultimately also an achievement of Luther. For the young Luther, as for the younger Robert and the still younger infant, Erikson writes as was quoted in the previous chapter: "The dominant issue of this as of any other stage, therefore, is the assurance that the active, the selective ego is in charge and enabled to be in charge by a social structure which grants a given age group the place it needs—and in which it is needed" (IY&C, 246).[10]

The Action Structure of Play

The difference in Erikson's description of self-formation derives from the greater emphasis placed upon the role of individual achievement and upon a growing awareness of individual competence. This difference, it is my contention, need not oppose Gadamer's emphasis upon the role of belonging to tradition and upon becoming aware of this belongingness. However, it was earlier observed how Gadamer's description of *Bildung* leads to the conclusion that the process is more event than action or more the action of the *Sache* than our action upon the *Sache*. Erikson avoids such a "more . . . than . . ." formulation of the relationship between adolescent and society, culture, history. This is because he includes what may be termed an "action structure" as being just as essential as Gadamer's happening structure to the description and comprehension of social play. It is useful to compare this action structure with what was earlier said about the event structure of *Bildung* and then explore the possible complementarity of both structures.

What is evident in Erikson's descriptions of childhood and social play is a deep concern for personal initiative that is not so much limited as enabled by social structure and, of course, by history and tradition as well. The block construction of the young boy Robert seeks to compensate for his present physical and social clumsiness by embedding a new identity element of physical and social wholeness "in a new sense of community." The personal initiative of the aspirant cockfighter is similarly directed toward forming a successful personal variation of a socially esteemed role. Even Luther's rebellion is interpreted in terms of preserving a Christian tradition rather than discarding it. Therefore Erikson writes in general of an interdependency between cultural striving and the individual aspiration of children and adolescents:

> Each new being is received into a style of life prepared by
> tradition and held together by tradition, and at the same
> time disintegrating because of the very nature of tradition.
> We say that tradition "molds" the individual, "channels" his
> drives. But the social process does not mold a new being
> merely to housebreak him; it molds generations in order to
> be remolded, to be reinvigorated, by them. . . . There is an
> optimum ego synthesis to which the individual aspires; and
> there is an optimal societal metabolism for which societies
> and cultures strive. In describing the interdependence of
> individual aspiration and of societal striving, we describe
> something indispensable to human life. [YML, 254]

In this interdependency between individual aspiration and societal striving, the individual is definitely a part of the larger process of socialization and cultural transmission as disclosed by Gadamer's concept of *wirkungsgeschichtliches Bewusstsein*, but it is an equally important consideration that the individual not be "housebroken" but rather actively contribute to the "remolding" or the "reinvigoration" of tradition. Thus the resolution of young Luther's life crisis is not only a historical and cultural event, but a personal act on his part that changes the tradition of which he is a part. The young Balinese male who aspires to be a true cockfighter is similarly seeking not only to imitate but also find his own style of training roosters. Even the block construction of the five-year-old is considered a creative renewal that exhibits "playful mastery in the present."

In each of these instances an "action structure" is evident in the description of the childhood or social play. This structure emphasizes different features in the process of play or self-formation than those described in chapter 2 concerning the happening structure of play. The action structure focuses on how the action has been enabled by the connection with tradition and family rather than how it is limited by the connection. Rather than the persistence of the event character of play, the novelty of the individual action, the uniqueness of the individual contribution, or the particularity of the personal identity is stressed. And crucial to the structure is the belief of the player that he or she can contribute or is capable of being a remolder or reinvigorator of the play.

Rather than the emphasis upon how the individual player is part of the larger, unfinished event of the game, the action structure stresses how the carrying out of the play is dependent upon the capabilities and activities of the player. Crucial to the establishment of this importance of the player is the specific phenomenon of childhood or adolescent social play, and how the child or adolescent is active in the construction of his block figure or in the formulation of his or her individual aspirations. More generally, the "action structure" of play differs from its "happening structure," insofar as it focuses on the contribution of the player to the game rather than on the to-and-fro movement of the play, and conveys how the way of being of play is such that the player not only "is played" but "plays" in individually characteristic ways.

However, in spite of this inversion of "all playing is a being played" (T&M, 95) to "all being played is a playing," Erikson's descriptions of childhood and social play do not subvert the original event characterization of play. They do not in any way imply that play is action "more than" event or that it is our action "alone." This is because Eriksonian *Bildung*, again if it can be designated as such, presents a balance between the aspiration of the individual, especially the adolescent in transition to adulthood, and the striving of the society, culture, tradition to which the individual belongs.

This interdependency of individual aspiration and cultural striving may be taken as an indication of the complementarity of both characterizations, of the action of individual education and personal appropriation of tradition, and of the larger event of *Bildung* and cultural transmission at the same time. A process of education or self-formation is described as both an event and an action, and is said to involve both belongingness to societal striving and achievement with respect to individual aspiration, with there being an interdependency or a balancing between the two rather than a subordinating or relegating relationship. Therefore the "action structure" of the Eriksonian description of play does not supplant or subvert, but only supplements Gadamer's event structure of play, understanding, and appropriation.

However, one issue of particularly immediate importance remains to be discussed, if the complementarity of Gadamer's happening structure and this proposed action structure is to be pursued with greater consequence. Gadamer's emphasis upon the happening structure of play, *Bildung*, and appropriation supports and is supported by his analysis of *wirkungsgeschichtliches Bewusstsein* as the consciousness of belonging to a hermeneutical situation and being part of an unfinished historical event. He opposes the power attributed by Habermas to self-reflection in *Knowledge and Human Interests*, insofar as this power to dissolve pseudo-natural constraints and to attain transparency in the self-formation process denies the role of hermeneutical situatedness. What sort of consciousness supports and is supported by a description of play, *Bildung*, and appropriation that emphasizes their action structure, and can this consciousness fit in with the thesis of hermeneutical situatedness?

In the next and final chapter, I will seek to articulate a consciousness of having been enabled that is supported by and supports Erikson's descriptions of childhood and adolescent play. I will also argue that this consciousness of enablement has a different, yet necessary, role in relation to the consciousness of having been effected by history and tradition.

Personal Appropriation and the Consciousness of Having Been Enabled

I n this chapter, Erik Erikson's descriptions of childhood play and the social play of adolescence will be linked with his accounts of the experience of basic trust in earliest childhood and of the attainment of ego integration in the final stage of the life cycle in order to show how the interdependency of cultural striving and individual aspiration continues throughout life. The linkage of these stages will, in an admittedly hermeneutically inspired and motivated reading of Erikson, help produce a narrative script that can be both comprehended as a generalized psychological theory for our culture and, more importantly from the point of view of this chapter, projected as an autobiography in a personal and particularized form.

One goal of this endeavor is to exhibit how the personal achievement aspect of the appropriation process does not simply refer to the attainment of identity in adolescence, but refers both backwards to the play and belongingness of childhood, and especially forward to the integration and completion of individual life history as a task of personal appropriation. The second goal of the narrative script is to convey how Erikson's description of the life cycle allows in its final stage for the becoming aware of having been enabled through the earliest stages of life so that an entire life history of both continuity and change can be appropriated in a deeply personal process.

This attention directed toward the appropriation of individual life history will make the treatment of the topic of appropriation quite different from that in the first chapter, which was devoted to the appropriation of history and tradition as precisely that which was not individual and exceeded the individual. With the great emphasis that has been placed upon the metaphor of balance in this study, it will come as no surprise that a balance between individual life history and the larger historical event will indeed be spoken of. However, it is also probably more necessary to motivate the acceptance of such a balance in this instance, because of the apparent ways that historical event and tradition do exceed individual biography. After the process of personal appropriation is explained in the first section by means of Erikson's description of the attainment of ego integrity in the final stage of the life cycle, the main events of the Ingmar Bergman film *Wild Strawberries* are narrated in the next section and then related to Erikson's analysis of them. Then the third section will attempt to provide this motivation, insofar as it takes up a kind of disproportion, evident in the film, that is different from that between the working out of history and individual consciousness—namely, the disparity between what has been willed to be done and what has in fact been accomplished.[1] This section will attempt to convey the importance of this different kind of disproportion and also to argue for the importance of a very different kind of experience from negative experience of reversal, namely a positive experience of enablement, in the reconciliation of this disparity.

Insofar as the Gadamer-Habermas debate, probably unwittingly and certainly unintentionally, offers the most recent and best confrontation on the issues of the nature and role of consciousness, it too will be brought into the context of the inquiry in the final section of this chapter, which concerns the consciousness accompanying the personal appropriation of Isak Borg, the film's main character. Because Dr. Borg's realization is a reflective one, it can be seen as an exercise in self-reflection and even, in early Habermasian terms, as an achievement of transparency in one's self-genesis. Since the realization ultimately involves the acceptance of death, it can involve in a more Gadamerian vein a recognition of "events that expose the littleness of knowing, feeling, doing—the littleness of subjectivity—in the face of the frightful immensity of what happens" (GH, 116). While there is much of value and importance in both of these descriptions of consciousness, I do not think it desirable to be put in a position of only having to consider them. Rather I will explore whether the description of another kind of consciousness can avoid the confrontation between historical belongingness and individual achievement, and support a more complementary and mutual relationship. My thesis will be that a description of consciousness can offer such support if it involves above all the recognition of how individual achievement has been enabled by historical belongingness rather than the awareness of subjective limitation or, conversely, the experience of personal emancipation.

Ego Integrity and the
Reasons of Old Age

The first very interesting facet in the attempt to articulate a conception of personal appropriation on the basis of Erikson's writings is that his most insightful and penetrating comments about the need for autobiographical perspective are made primarily in regard to adolescence, as we have already seen, and in regard to the final stage of his life cycle, ego integration, and not in regard to the intermediate stages of adulthood between adolescence and old age. Adulthood in general is characterized as a period in which the panic caused by an earlier identity crisis and the anxiety before an impending death are avoided. Rather "usually on the basis of a function in an economy, a place in the sequence of generations, and a status in the structure of society" (YML, 111–12), a more or less "automatic recourse"[2] is developed toward contexts where the adult is needed or recognized by others as he or she recognizes them or has mastered some skill or technique that brings obvious and culturally recognized returns. For the adult, "the past is part of a present mastery which employs a convenient mixture of forgetting, falsifying and idealizing to fit the past to the present" (YML, 217); it "is not an inexorable process experienced only as preparation for an impending doom" (YML, 217) as it might be either for a youth in crisis or an aged person before death.

Thus it is primarily in old age and in adolescence that there is the possibility of an "ego-chill, a shudder which comes from the sudden awareness of our non-existence" (YML, 111), that can shock one into a more pronounced state of self-awareness. In youth the fear is that some social or biological force is hopelessly determining the past and present. Erikson writes in *Identity: Youth and Crisis* of the development of historical perspective in youth:

> [It is] a sense of the irreversibility of significant events and an often urgent need to understand fully and quickly what kind of happenings in reality and in thought determine others, and why. As we have seen, psychologists such as Piaget recognize in youth the capacity to appreciate that any process can be understood when it is retraced in its steps and thus reversed in thought. Yet it is no contradiction to say that he who comes to understand such a reversal also realizes that in reality, among all the events that can be thought of, a few will determine and narrow one another with historical fatality, whether (in the human instance) deservedly or undeservedly, intentionally or unintentionally. [IY&C, 247]

Therefore the goal of retracing the past is to oppose this sense of irreversibility of events by developing a life plan for the future that is one's own and avoids the feared fatalism.

The crisis of old age, even if occasioned by the fear of an impending death, is necessarily less future-oriented and more directed to the past. As Erikson explains in *Young Man Luther*:

> The *crisis of generativity* occurs when a man looks at what he has generated, or helped to generate, and finds it good or wanting, when his life work as part of the productivity of his time gives him some sense of being on the side of a few angels or makes him feel stagnant. All this, in turn, offers him either promise of an old age that can be faced with a sense of integrity, and in which he can say, "All in all, I would do this over again," or confronts him with a sense of waste, of despair. [YML, 243]

Hence the reasons of old age revolve around the attainment of a historical perspective through "to be, through having been," just as the play of the child and the social play of the adolescent are modeled upon the mastery of future experiences.

Erikson's sense of being through having been is entirely complementary with Gadamer's historically effected consciousness, but it depends upon two different ways of belonging. As for Gadamer, the task of old age involves for Erikson the recognition of being a part of one's history, one's culture, one's generation in a biological and historical succession of generations. However, in addition to this uncompleted history and cycle of generations, there is an individual life that one is also situated in and that is in fact nearing completion. It is in relation to both these cycles that the task of the final stage of the individual life cycle is situated. Erikson designates the crisis at the end of life, as alluded to above, a crisis of integrity whose successful outcome is "the detached and yet active concern with life itself in the face of death itself" (BLC, 26) and that "maintains and conveys the integrity of experience" (BLC, 26) in spite of disdain over human failings and the dread of death. The stage is, then, ego integrity, a state of mind of being whole, entire, complete. The attainment of this sense of wholeness, entirety, and completion is dependent on not only fulfilling and completing one's life but on contributing to one's place in the larger cycles of history: "Any fulfillment of the individual life cycle, far from being simply a matter of finding terminal clarity, can only fulfill what is given in the order of things by remaining responsible and by contributing continuous solutions to the ongoing cycle of generations" (BLC, 29).

Erikson's longer description of ego integrity, which first appears in *Childhood and Society* and is often repeated in other books and articles, describes a process of "final consolidation" of both the individual life cycle and the larger segment of history of which the individual life is a part:

> Lacking a clear definition, I shall point to a few constituents of this state of mind [ego integrity]. It is the ego's accrued assurance of its proclivity for order and meaning. It is a post-narcissistic love of the human ego—not of the self—as an experience which conveys some world order and spiritual sense, no matter how dearly paid for. It is the acceptance of one's one and only life cycle as something that had to be and that, by necessity, permitted of no substitutions: it thus means a new, a different love of one's parents. It is a comradeship with the ordering ways of distant times and different pursuits, as expressed in the simple products and sayings of such times and pursuits. Although aware of the relativity of all the various life styles which have given meaning to human striving, the possessor of integrity is ready to defend the dignity of his own life style against all physical and economic threats. For he knows that an individual life is the accidental coincidence of but one life cycle with but one segment of history; and that for him all human integrity stands or falls with the one style of integrity of which he partakes. The style of integrity developed by his culture or civilization thus becomes the "patrimony of his soul," the seal of his moral paternity of himself (". . . pero el honor / Es patrimonio del alma": Calderon). In such final consolidation, death loses its sting. [C&S, 268]

The Remarkable Events of Dr. Borg's Journey in *Wild Strawberries*

Rather than commenting on all the constituents of ego integrity—a task to which I do not feel myself capable—I will focus my attention in the next two sections upon the process of consolidation itself and even there not so much on its relation to the dread of death as on the role that experience of a positive kind can play in the completion or fulfillment of the process. My guide in this endeavor is

Erikson's analysis of what I believe is both an event and action of final consolidation by Isak Borg, the main figure in Ingmar Bergman's film *Wild Strawberries*. If the principal comparison in the previous chapter was between Gadamer's description of play and Erikson's description of child's play, the implicit comparison here is between Gadamer's analysis of experience in *Truth and Method* and the experience Erikson points to and analyzes in a film involving "modern self-analysis."

Isak Borg is a seventy-six-year-old Swedish doctor, a widower, the father of one married but childless son. He is to receive in the ancient cathedral of the city of Lund the highest award of his profession, a jubilee doctorate marking fifty years of meritorious service. Despite this official recognition of outstanding accomplishment, he is someone who is indifferent, selfish, and troubled by his life.

The film narrates the events of Dr. Borg's car trip from his place of retirement to Lund, the ceremony wherein he receives his award, and some moments of memory and reflection that follow the ceremony. The ceremony itself is experienced as something superficial and meaningless; but Borg remembers the events of the day during the ceremony and decides to write them down, for "I was beginning to see a remarkable causality in this chain of unexpected, entangled events" (IB, 233). Erikson terms this pronouncement a "revelatory sensation of grand simplicity" (BLC, 16). The revelation involves not just a car trip but a journey by which we are "led from the compulsive rituals of a lonely old man through some everyday ritualizations of culture, to a grand ritual which both seals and permits a transcendence of his over-defined professional life" (BLC, 2). If Dr. Borg indeed achieves a transcendence of his professional life, it is because, in Erikson's terminology, he is able to achieve a "final consolidation," a new personal appropriation of his life events.

In the sequence of events before the awards ceremony, Borg encounters all the elements of the earlier described generativity crisis.[3] He recognizes a feeling of stagnation, he finds that what he has generated is wanting, and he even comes to sense both his isolation and despair. In a dream on the evening before the day of the ceremony, he witnesses on his "usual morning stroll" a hearse that crashes in front of him, depositing its coffin, which opens and reveals the doctor's own face. Erikson's analysis is: "The viewer's first impression is that the dream tries to tell the dreamer—is it 'merely' because of his advancing age or in view of the approaching 'crowning' event in his life, or for some other reason?—that he must not permit his official and so isolated self to beckon him into the grave. Perhaps he must as yet learn to die?" (BLC, 5).

After being startled by the dream, Borg awakens and spontaneously decides to travel to Lund by car rather than, as earlier planned, by plane. He is joined in his trip by his daughter-in-law, Marianne, who, having been awakened by the commotion, also quickly decides to join him. During the first part of the trip, "she elaborates on the fact that she has now stayed with him a month with the 'idiotic idea' that he may help Evald [her husband and Borg's son] and her, but that he had refused adamantly to hear about their marital trouble, suggesting that maybe she needs a quack or a minister" (BLC, 6). He in turn wants to tell her of his dream, but she expresses a lack of interest. Erikson's "clinical impressions" conclude: "In her, a strong ethical determination seems to have been awakened that the future must not be forfeited to what is dead in the Borgs' past, even as Borg's old-age struggle against despair makes him comprehend that what he has become must not be all that he is and must not be all that he leaves behind" (BLC, 7).

Borg then makes an unplanned detour in the trip by taking a side road to the summer home of his childhood. Marianne goes down to the water for a swim while he proceeds to the strawberry patch in front of the house where he lies down and dreams of events in childhood: losing his "first love" in competition with his older brother and a gathering of the extended family. In Erikson's analysis, "didactically speaking, this childhood scene would permit us, step by step, to sketch the way in which, in comparison to the others, Isak resolved his childhood crises by acquiring some specialized strengths that would later serve him well in a professional career in his cultural setting, but for which he would have to pay with a certain compulsive self-restriction that began to possess him early" (BLC, 9).

Several further events during the trip serve to make manifest to Borg this self-constriction. He and Marianne visit his mother, alive and still alert, but isolated by her own coldness and estranged from the living members of her family except for Evald. Returning to the car, Marianne resumes the driving and Borg dreams again of his childhood sweetheart with his brother, but this scene is interrupted when he is taken into a lecture room and examined by the male figure from a married couple who had been picked up earlier on the car trip but who were so unpleasant that they had to be asked to leave. In the examination, Borg is found guilty of "indifference, selfishness, lack of consideration" (IB, 218). This verdict is confirmed in the next scene of the dream where Borg witnesses his wife's infidelity to him that is brought on by his own indifference. Again Erikson's analysis is that "Isak, who has learned how to study, to heal, and to preserve life, has not been alive to a woman's or his own feelings, and so he has had to watch the women in his life, although they loved him, turn to other men" (BLC, 14).

Borg awakens from his dream and tells his daughter-in-law what his dreams appear to tell him: "That I'm dead, although I live" (IB, 223). She responds in a way that confirms Erikson's earlier observation about her determination to keep the future from being forfeit to the Borgs' past.[4] She tells Borg that her husband had said much the same thing to her at the end of a dramatic conversation they had had when she had announced her pregnancy: he had said that she had a need to live and create life while he had a need to be dead. Moreover she was frightened by the coldness of Borg's mother. As he now listens very carefully, she tells him of her decision to have the child, no matter what her husband feels, and looks at Borg with a "black, accusing, desperate" (IB, 227) gaze. He in turn "suddenly felt shaken" in a way he "had never experienced before" (IB, 227).

These are the events preceding the awards ceremony with the "remarkable causality" and that produce, in Erikson's terms, an "ego-chill." After the ceremony, they are followed by a dream or a memory that is even more "remarkable" from Erikson's point of view toward the life cycle. Before falling asleep, Borg's attention "wanders back" to childhood memories of the summer home. He and his childhood sweetheart are going out to look for his parents whom Isak could not find by himself. Walking to a narrow sound of water, they come to see an older man fishing on the other side and, farther up the bank, an older woman reading. The younger Isak tries to shout to them but no word is said; his father recognizes him and first he waves and then Isak's mother nods her head. Isak also recognizes his uncle and his siblings and friends, and shouts to them but without their hearing. At the end of the final scene of the film, he says: "I dreamed that I stood by the water and shouted toward the bay, but the warm summer breeze carried away my cries and they did not reach their destination. Yet I wasn't sorry about that; I felt, on the contrary, rather light-hearted" (IB, 239).

The Role of Positive Experience in Borg's Self-Analysis

Erikson refers, as was quoted above, to Borg's inner journey as a "grand ritual which both seals and permits a transcendence of his over-defined professional existence." Of the notion of ritual, he writes, "there can be no prescription for either ritualization or ritual, for, far from being merely repetitive or familiar in the sense of habituation, any true ritualization, while ontogenetically grounded, is yet pervaded with the spontaneity of surprise: it is an unexpected renewal of a recognizable order in potential chaos" (T&R, 113). It is the experience of protected childhood play at the beginning of his life that Borg both consciously comes to recognize and, if I am not mistaken, is at the same time an unexpected surprise for him.

If Borg feels lighthearted in recollecting an early experience from childhood, it is not because the experience is not profound according to Erikson. However, it is profoundly different from the kind of experience that is given the most prominent role in Gadamer's philosophical hermeneutics. That description of the nature of experience refers, as we have seen, "chiefly to painful and disagreeable experiences" (T&M, 319), to disappointments of expectations that result from experience acquired without being sought or intended. Experience for Gadamer is primarily of negativity and its role, like that of *wirkungsgeschichtliches Bewusstsein*, is to make us aware of our finitude and open to the workings of history.

Dr. Borg has had experiences of this Gadamerian kind. He is aware of his impending death and, in all likelihood, open to his tradition that is working within him (even officially recognizing him). Concerning his own attitude toward this recognition, it certainly appears to be one of someone who has learned, in the earlier quoted words of Weinsheimer, "not any particular thing, but rather the uncertainty of all plans and predictions, the frustrations of all attempts to control or close off the future, and the disappointment of all aspirations to comprehend in a single concept, however inclusive, the infinite process of experience" (GH, 204–5).

However, if Borg is disturbed at the beginning of *Wild Strawberries* by a crisis of generativity, this crisis is the result of experiences of reversal and disappointment that are more personal in nature than those described by Weinsheimer. They involve not a disproportion between Borg's achievements and the larger historical events he is caught up in, but rather the disproportion between actual personal achievement and what had been hoped and willed to be achieved by Borg himself. There is profound disappointment in the personal decisions and actions he has made rather than in their inherent limitations, and intense regret that the personal reversals in his life can no longer be reversed.

From the historical perspective that the main character of *Wild Strawberries* begins with and is confirmed by all his earlier reminiscences, Borg fears that his entire life must be an irreversible series of personal mistakes and disappointments. Nevertheless the final stop in his journey involves a memory of a "truly primal scene" of parental protection and an experience of positivity and surprise rather than such negativity and disappointment. It is, in Erikson's terms, a scene of "basic trust." This sense of trust is primarily unconscious[5] and begins to be acquired by the infant in its first encounters with its mother and other primary caretakers. Such basic trust is to be achieved by a "human being which at the beginning wants, in addition to the fulfillment of oral and sensory needs, to be gazed upon by the primal parent and to respond to the gaze, to look up to the parental countenance and to be responded to, continues to look up, and to look for somebody to look up to, and that is somebody who will, in the very act of returning his glance, lift him up" (T&R, 91). Thus it is a sense of original belongingness in early childhood that at the same time allows wider spheres of belongingness to develop from it. Erikson writes of basic trust that it "forms the basis in the child for a sense of identity which will later combine a sense of being 'all right,' of being oneself, and of becoming what other people trust one will become" (C&S, 249).[6]

At the same time that the "primal scene" is imbued with such strong elements of belongingness, it is nonetheless a scene with an equal place for mastery and achievement. The earlier events in *Wild Strawberries* already reveal the power of memory to make Borg aware of his professional accomplishments and personal failures. Yet the "remarkable causality of events" that has allowed him in his old age to remember the achievements and failures forgotten in adulthood also leads back to an original scene of protected childhood play as "the infantile form of the human ability to deal with experience by creating model situations and to master reality by experiment and planning" (C&S, 222). As the young boy Robert in his construction of childhood blocks attains a "promised renewal" and avoids "the recapitulation of possible doom" through playful mastery in the present, so Borg now renews and reenacts his experience of earlier play in a manner in which he hopes to avoid the recapitulation of his "overdefined professional existence." In Erikson's earlier words, "no thinker can do more and no playing child less" (C&S, 222).

If pace Gadamer we learn *from* negative experience and recognize thereby our limitations in the face of history, we also learn according to Erikson *through* and *because of* positive experience in regard to our personal lives. What Borg learns through his positive experience of basic trust is how he has been protected and helped from the beginning of his life. What he learns because of this experience is how this protection and help have enabled him to be the capable and accomplished, the *gebildete* human being that he is. Thus what Borg becomes conscious of is both that he has already been helped in a process of self-formation and that he is and has been enabled to be competent—to play, to learn—and to be capable—to develop, to *change*. The positive experience of basic trust and early agency, an experience of having earlier been enabled to be the subject that one is, can be capable of altering the effect of negative personal experiences of disappointment, perhaps even of an entire life.

For Erikson the task of final consolidation presented to Borg is to find continuity between the positive experience of play in childhood and the experiences of both professional success and personal failure later in life. Within the context of this process of integration, the negative experiences of disappointment and failure are extremely important to Borg; however, it is only by remembering the positive scene of protected play from childhood that he "redeems his failures and strengthens his hopes" (C&S, 222). It is only through the addition of this positive experience into a new and now completed historical perspective that he "anticipates the future from the point of view of a corrected and shared past" (C&S, 222). Therefore for Erikson the experiences of both belonging in a relationship of basic trust and of being enabled thereby to achieve are not opposed to and may even reconcile the experiences of disappointment and limitation in regard to one's social assignments and personal accomplishments. Dr. Borg can appropriate the significant events of his life history in the literal sense of make them his own because of the continuity found between the initial events of his childhood, the ensuing shortcomings of his life, and finally his new hopes and aspirations for personal change.

The Consciousness of Having Been Enabled

Erikson praises Ingmar Bergman for his art "that permits him to depict a variety of persons of different ages in acute life crises in a sequence of short scenes which typify the whole course of their lives so vividly that we viewers are sure we have 'met' them" (BLC, 3) and, above all, for his intuition that allows him as a middle-age filmmaker to portray so convincingly the crises of old age. In my estimate, the praise also redounds upon Erikson and his own achievement of intuition as well. The essay on *Wild Strawberries* indicates how his description of the completed life cycle can be used in a manner other than as a theoretical construct to be compared with Habermas's theoretical account of the development of ego identity; namely, as a retrospective narrative of the past and as an anticipatory narrative for the future. The complete description of the life cycle requires a projection into the future similar to the conclusion of Bergman's film, and Erikson achieves this projection not just theoretically in his description of the final stage of ego integration but personally in the anticipation of his own life's end. The profound description of this projection into the future does not oppose Gadamer's equally profound description, as we have seen, of the thrownness in the past and of our hermeneutical situatedness in history. However, even as Gadamer's *wirkungsgeschichtliches Bewusstsein* attests to the disproportion between human consciousness and the working out of the event of history and tradition, so does Erikson's final stage of the life cycle provide personal insight into the power of the consciousness of having been enabled to address the disproportion between what is willed to be done and what is in fact accomplished.

If my conjecture is correct, Erikson's narration of the events in the human life cycle is based not only on the script of a fictional movie character or on clinical observations, but also on his own both experienced past and projected future life events. In this respect, there can be said to be a personal situatedness in Erikson's description of the psychosocial life cycle that is comparable in certain ways to the personal situatedness and individual accomplishment of Sigmund Freud's self-analysis. It is useful to compare this conjectured "personal" life analysis of Erikson with aspects of Freud's documented self-analysis, in part to relate what at least may be inferred about the subject of consciousness from an Eriksonian perspective to Habermas's conception of self-reflection, inspired as it is by his interpretation of Freudian analysis.

Despite all the claims of continuity on Erikson's part, his style of self-examination, of which of course I am in part only conjecturing, also differs from Freud's self-analysis and his analysis of other patients. One very striking difference lies in the fact that Erikson can refer to the concluding scene of *Wild Strawberries* as a "truly primal scene" and clearly mean by this phrase something quite different from Freud. On the one hand, for Freud (and for Lorenzer and Habermas as well) there is the primal scene of original repression with its accompanying compulsion toward repetition; on the other hand, Erikson describes a primal scene of childhood play that is protected by parents. Another difference, which Erikson explicitly mentions, is the psychosexual nature of the Freudian sequence of development and the psychosocial character of the Eriksonian life cycle. A final difference relates to the temporal orientation that is emphasized in each of these sequences. The incontestable greatness of Freud's self-analysis lies in the achievement of overcoming resistances to the memory of important past repressed events. If there is any similar degree of accomplishment on the part of Erikson, as I am inclined to think there is, it lies, with Bergman, in the capability to project into the future to describe a whole life history. Thus whereas Freud seeks by reflection in his self-analysis to overcome the repression that is inherent in the primal scene as he conceives it, Erikson explains how to become conscious of a whole life of continuity with, change from, and development, preservation, and completion of the primal scene of protected childhood playfulness.

The purpose of this comparison between Freud and Erikson is in no way to set up an opposition between styles of psychoanalytic practice that I believe, in fact, to be thoroughly complementary.[7] Rather it is to point out from what is now the very rich context of what may broadly be termed the psychoanalytic tradition a conception of consciousness that is not immediately directed toward the overcoming of pseudo-natural constraints or to the attainment of complete self-transparency. To become conscious of the experience of parental trust and the mastery of childhood play does not involve—as it well might for a traumatic childhood event (for which, of course, Habermas's conception of self-reflection is more pertinent)—the desire to overcome its quasi-natural and unconscious nature, but rather the insight to preserve or renew the belief in having been enabled through the youthful crises of adolescence, the engagements and demands of adulthood, and the situation before death. If Habermas observes that, as quoted above in chapter 4, we can "have an orientation to the future, which makes it possible for the past to become a problem" (TCA2, 106), Erikson's description of orientation toward the future in old age is such that the past can offer its only solution.

For Habermas, the "act of self-reflection that 'changes a life' is a movement of emancipation" (K&HI, 212). The consciousness of having been enabled is not, if my interpretation of the change in Borg's life is accurate, in itself such a form or activity of mastery understood as emancipation. Rather than an awareness of overcoming social constraint or instinctual repression, it is a consciousness of a positive experience of enablement with an accompanying sense of individual mastery and agency. If it "changes a life," it does so through the preservation of, development from and, at a certain stage of life, completion of the original experience of enablement. Hence the act of becoming conscious of having been enabled includes a consciousness of mastery as a most essential aspect, but it is conceived of in terms of preservation and development, and not liberation.

Moreover, the sense of mastery that the consciousness of having been enabled supports does not necessarily oppose the emphasis on finitude so prominent in Gadamer's philosophical hermeneutics. Isak Borg does not want to liberate himself from all past history and tradition. Nor does he aspire to the power and will to place it completely under his conscious control. Rather it is *his* history he would like to believe he could master in some way, *his* life he would like to know he could change, *his* isolation he would like to bring to an end.

What happens to him, as depicted in the conclusion of *Wild Strawberries* and also more generally in Erikson's description of final consolidation, is that he becomes conscious of being an actor in his life and experiences an openness to new possibilities of his own willing and control. This consciousness of being able to change a previously feared inevitability does not rival or substitute for the consciousness of being an effect of history or, in the new translation, of being a historically effected consciousness. Indeed Borg refers to a "remarkable causality" of a "chain of unexpected, entangled events," even as he attains a new ability to change the direction of the personal events of his life.

Nevertheless it would be an insufficient description to say that the revelation Borg experiences is a happening to him and an inaccurate description to classify it an event "more than" an action. Because of the events of his remarkable journey, he renews his will and redeems his purpose. But concerning the journey itself, he is both, to use vocabulary from Gadamer's *Truth and Method*, the leader of it and the led. He discovers not only that he is "always already" situated in history, but also that he "always already" has acted with will and purpose (even before his conscious awareness). Thus he recognizes that the events of his past life are at the same time a series of personal actions that can be reversed and he projects his future death as a final event and action that he will both suffer and accept. The event of revelation is at the same time a personal act of recognition that all his actions have been enabled by history and that he is still able to act in his own history, even to its end.

The kind of consciousness that is implicated in this description of final consolidation as it is applied to the film *Wild Strawberries* is above all one of the complementarity and mutuality of individual action and historical event, of personal achievement and historical belongingness. The life history begins with a primal scene of belongingness to an intimate family circle and yet also with a sense of the

early capabilities of and achievement in play. The sphere of belongingness extends in the subsequent events of childhood, just as the
sense of competence and accomplishment also grows. In adolescence
there is the youthful expression of both rebellion and fidelity, while
in adulthood there is both cultural consolidation and personal initiative. The final consolidation in old age is no different, as Borg learns
to look at death as the final event *and* the final action of his life.

As pointed out in the previous section, the consciousness of
having been enabled issues from a different kind of experience than
is usually emphasized in philosophical hermeneutics. This experience
is not a negative one of limitation that leads to and supports both the
consciousness of finitude and the finitude of consciousness. Rather it
is a positive experience of having been enabled to achieve: by the
protection of parents, by the socialization process of a dynamic social
structure, and also by the tradition to which we belong. Thus what is
preserved in consciousness is, in distinction to the consciousness of
having been effected, *both* a sense of belongingness to family and
tradition *and* a feeling of individual mastery enabled by that same
belongingness.

Therefore this consciousness of enablement does not oppose
the profound importance of historical situatedness as it is developed
by Gadamer, but only the definite and deliberate rhetorical thrust in
Truth and Method that is expressed in statements like "the self-awareness of the individual is only a flickering in the closed circuits of
historical life" (T&M, 245). It would be a change—and indeed a
profound change—if the thrust of these rhetorical comments were to
be dropped in favor of a complementarity between historical belongingness and individual aspiration, and in allowance of a conception of
the consciousness of personal appropriation that recognizes a major
and equal role for personal achievement.

We do experience the disproportion between our subjectivity
and the larger working out of history that is so clearly alluded to in
the above rhetorical comment, but we also experience the personal
disproportion between what we will to do and what we actually
accomplish. Concerning the first disproportion, there is a consciousness of history that is "always at work" and even a consciousness of
being effected by history. Concerning the second disproportion,
however, there may also be, we may hope, the disclosure of a
consciousness of personal achievement that is "always at work" in our
lives, that has already been enabled by the events of our life histories,
and that can allow us to believe that we can change the directions of
our life histories. I believe the narration of Dr. Borg's integration of
personal history in *Wild Strawberries* and Erikson's more general

description of the process of final consolidation to be of equal significance to Gadamer's discussion of historically effected consciousness and the truth that is appropriated through it. To become cognizant of both "consciousnesses" and the different important roles that they play in life history and the larger event of tradition is to gain awareness of how we are both products of our tradition and initiators within that tradition at the same time. Indeed this is what Borg's process of personal appropriation finally consolidates in a manner that he can both gratefully and meaningfully accept, insofar as he becomes conscious of and even surprised by the positive experience of being already enabled to be an individual within a tradition that at the same time has made him the individual that he is. The important senses of agency, will, and purpose that he recognizes through his consciousness of having been enabled ought also to be acknowledged by philosophical hermeneutics, even if this acknowledgment compromises well-known polemical comparisons.

Conclusion

The Prehistory of
Personal Achievement

I have attempted to explicate a consciousness of having been enabled and to argue for its inclusion into the context of philosophical hermeneutics as a necessary and useful complement to Gadamer's description of the consciousness of having been historically effected. Such a consciousness of having been enabled is supported by and itself supports descriptions of the same processes that have such a central role in *wirkungsgeschichtliches Bewusstsein*: play, *Bildung*, appropriation, and self-understanding. The difference is that the consciousness of enablement depends upon the Eriksonian descriptions of these processes, which emphasize the mastery involved, that they are or are on the way toward being personal achievements, whereas *wirkungsgeschichtliches Bewusstsein* orientates itself upon the Gadamerian emphasis on the situatedness or belongingness at work, which is expressed in terms of the happening structure of the process. Thus what is necessary to effect an integration of both consciousnesses is to put forward descriptions of play, *Bildung*, and appropriation as both historical events and personal achievements without a necessary priority being assigned to either aspect.

I indeed believe that Gadamer's happening structure of play and Erikson's action structure of play are complementary and equal descriptions of the same phenomenon. However, the arguments for the cogency of Erikson's description of childhood play and for the importance of the action structure within this description rest ultimately upon the importance of the phenomenon of childhood play in comparison to adult play, and the issue of that importance in itself is a difficult matter to assess. One of Paul Ricoeur's many important accomplishments in his reading of Sigmund Freud, *Sigmund Freud: An Essay on Interpretation*, is to have pointed toward a difficult problem and indeed even a limit for the applicability of phenomenology: How is a method developed for the description of the intentional activities of consciousness to gain access to the description of the unconscious, its operations and mechanisms? Although the distinction between childhood play and adult play is of course less dramatic than Freud's distinction, it has some of the same implications for the application of phenomenological method. For phenomenologists have not only presupposed the conscious exercise of their methods upon the conscious acts they have wished to describe, but also the "mature" exercise of their methods upon typically adult activities as well. In the Foreword to the second edition of *Truth and Method*, Gadamer states that he is offering phenomenological descriptions of both play and conversation that are open to the standards of assessment for phenomenology (T&M, xxiv). The issue is whether these standards for the phenomenological description of play are adequate, if the distinction between childhood play and adult play is not made and taken seriously in the formulation of the play description.

I believe that the distinction between childhood and adult play is indeed very important and that the acknowledgment of the action structure of childhood play forms the basis for the argument for the general importance of the action structure of play. Nevertheless I also feel that to insist upon the distinction between childhood and adult play has the additional unfortunate and unintended effect of neglecting the feature of Erikson's analysis of play that is actually the most pertinent in the comparison with Gadamer's philosophical hermeneutics and the event structure of play. That feature is the close interrelationship, not distinctness, that Erikson finds between childhood play and adult work and recreation, and it is to this feature that I wish to return in the conclusion of this study.

Erik Erikson attributes such a central role to his analysis of childhood play that he speaks of it as the "royal road" (*via regia*) to his discoveries in an explicit comparison with Freud: "To Freud, the *via regia* to mental life had been the dream. For me, children's play became the first *via regia* to an understanding of growing man's conflicts and triumphs, his repetitive working through of the past, and his creative self-renewal in truly playful moments" (LHHM, 39). What is crucial in this quotation is not only the importance attributed to childhood play, but how this play is immediately related to the struggles, the work, and the creative self-renewal of adulthood. The same immediate relationship is established in the statement of his theory of childhood play from *Childhood and Society*, which is repeated here in full quotation:

> I propose the theory that the *child's* play is the infantile form of the human ability to deal with experience by creating model situations and to master reality by experiment and planning. It is in certain phases of his work that the *adult* projects past experience into dimensions which seem manageable. In the laboratory, on the stage, and on the drawing board, he relives the past and thus relieves leftover affects; in reconstructing the model situation, he redeems his failures and strengthens his hopes. He anticipates the future from the point of view of a corrected and shared past.
>
> No thinker can do more and no playing child less. [C&S, 222, italics added]

Contained within the final sentence of this quotation is an "awesome suggestion," which Erikson also makes in another context when writing of the adult division between play and recreation. There he states: "Such a division makes life simpler and permits adults to avoid the awesome suggestion that playfulness . . . may occur in the vital center of adult concerns, as it does in the center of those of children" (T&R, 18). This suggestion goes against adult pretensions about the distinctive importance of their work as opposed to "mere" play and against a developmental bias couched in terms of growth and maturation. Instead it suggests an importance to be attributable to childhood and playfulness, which "serious" and "mature" adults are prone to resist.

However, the suggestion does far more than convey the importance of playfulness; it has its awesome character from the fact that it suggests the need to preserve the playfulness of childhood play. In this respect there can be an analogy made to the "awesome suggestion"— of course far more than a suggestion—of Hans-Georg Gadamer about the need to preserve the consciousness of historical connectedness to tradition for the historical sciences (the *Geisteswissenschaften*) and for our own *Bildung*. Erikson is suggesting the need to preserve the playfulness of childhood play at the core of personal history in a manner analogous to Gadamer's preservation of our situatedness in history at large.

This suggestion relates to the feature of the consciousness of having been enabled that has not yet been sufficiently explicated—the "having been" in the "having been enabled." By this feature I mean the fact that the consciousness of enablement can be said to have its own "being" (*Sein*) as well as its consciousness (*Bewusstsein*). This "being" derives from the "preachievement" character of childhood play that gives it an analogous status in regard to adult achievement as Gadamer's notion of "prejudice" has in regard to conscious judgment. What Erikson's "big words for wordless play" reveal is a way of conceiving childhood play so that it is at the heart of a prehistory of personal achievement, not a nonhistory or a history of nonachievement. Examples of childhood play occupy within the larger personal history the role of individual preachievements on the way toward later personal accomplishments.

The prehistory of personal achievement depends upon a need for protection, which begins with the basic trust of infancy and extends to an allowance for and the toleration of the social play of adolescents. Such protection allows for the formation of "model situations"— situations for preactions or perhaps even rehearsals— which involve the anticipation of future achievements through meditating, experimenting, planning, and sharing in the present. It also has as perhaps the most important task the encouragement of a present sense of being competent to play and learn, and of being capable to develop greater future competency and independence.

What Erikson's "awesome suggestion" consists in is the implication that these preachievements brought about by the positive experience of basic trust and childhood play are just as important to individuals as their later accomplishments. Thus his contention that no adult thinker can do more and no playing child can do less carries out the same function on the level of this individual life history of achievement as Gadamer's conception of *wirkungsgeschichtliches Bewusstsein* effects toward the working out of effective history. It makes the life cycle into a historical process for the individual with both preservation and development, renewal and creativity, a "truth" that both continues and changes. It also situates subjectivity within that process, the only difference to Gadamer deriving from the fact that subjectivity is situated into a context of preachievement in childhood as well as into a context of prejudgment in respect to tradition. The "achievement history" contained within Erikson's description of the life cycle demonstrates that enablement has to itself "always already" be enabled in the same way that Gadamer demonstrates that conscious historical understanding has to be "always already" understood.

The preachievements of childhood play enable the later accomplishments of adult work and recreation because of their character as model situations. They also are themselves enabled by the protection, encouragement, and education of family and tradition. The "having been" in the consciousness of having been enabled involves the awareness of this enabling and enabled character of preachievement, an awareness that connects later personal achievement and conscious subjective action to its own prehistory and connects that prehistory to family and tradition. Therefore the consciousness of having been enabled entails the recognition that the thus enabled and enabling prehistory of achievement connects with other periods in individual life history as a period as important as any other.

This perspective toward childhood play that accords it as preachievement with a status equal to that of the later stages of the life cycle allows for a different reading of Erikson's life cycle than is usually the case with other, more theoretical models. This reading may even be termed, I wish to argue, a "hermeneutics of life history" that ought to be seen and needs to be recognized as a counterweight to the "theoretics of individual development" in schemes of rational reconstruction by philosophers like Habermas and psychologists like Piaget.

The phrase "life history" is appropriate in regard to Erikson's description of the stages of the life cycle, insofar as the "having been" in the consciousness of enablement does establish both a historical connection to an individual past and a sense of personal history. Ian Craib makes the point more specifically about Erikson's concept of identity, though it holds true for the entire life cycle that it "involves the passing of time: some sense of being able to integrate the past, the present and the future; and because of that it is something in continual development, over a lifetime, taking on new dimensions and depths" (P&ST, 78).

Moreover this kind of Eriksonian personal history displays many of the same features that have prominence in Gadamer's description of the working out of history. As explained above, the preachievements of different childhood stages are not interpreted as developmentally inferior actions, but simply as "different from" adult accomplishments and valuable nonetheless because of their role in the individual's prehistory leading to a history of action, achievement, and accomplishment. Thus the proper reading of the entire life cycle is not one of only progression in theoretical ability and development in cognitive and interactive skill, but rather one with an equally prominent aspect of preservation of past positive experience and the acknowledgment of continuity between life periods. In short, it has the same features as Gadamer's *Wirkungsgeschichte* in regard to the larger process of appropriation of tradition, only in this instance the concern is with the

personal appropriation of a life history of preachievement and achievement.

Finally, there is even a hermeneutical approach to
life history that is deeply akin to Gadamer's own conception of philosophical hermeneutics. At the conclusion of
Part One of *Truth and Method*, this conception is distinguished from that of Schleiermacher. Schleiermacher,
according to Gadamer, conceives of the purpose of
hermeneutics as "a second creation, the reproduction of
the original production" (T&M, 148-49), "the historical
reconstruction of a once living world" (GH, 131). He
sides with Hegel against Schleiermacher, because
"Hegel affirms difference as the condition of, rather
than obstacle to, assimilation and appropriation" (GH,
131). Essential, therefore, to the Gadamerian conception of hermeneutics is the affirmation that "Hegel
states a decisive truth in that the essence of historical
spirit consists not in the restitution of the past but rather
in thoughtful mediation with present life" (T&M, 150).

Erikson, too, is clearly concerned with the thoughtful
mediation of present life rather than any restitution of
an original past. Only in his instance the inquiry is into
the mediation of life history, and the integration with a
personal past of preachievement and enablement is
being preferred to a reconstruction of immature development. Like Gadamer, the prehistory of childhood is
the condition of, rather than obstacle to, integration.
And the process of integration that Erikson affirms
preserves the differences of this personal prehistory in
relationship to the present, even as it also establishes a
deep continuity between personal past, present, and
future. Indeed the one and only profound difference
between Gadamer's description of mediation and his
description of integration is that mediation is described
in terms of its event structure alone or event "more
than" action, while Erikson attributes an equal and
prominent role to "the sort of integration that a person
can achieve, a person's ability to see and perhaps understand personal experience in terms of their life as a
whole, as it has been in the past and it might be in the
future" (P&ST, 86).

The insight into the potential integration of life
history is one that, in my estimation, allows what has

earlier been called "hermeneutically informed and hermeneutically situated social science" to complement the progressive reconstructions of individual development outside the context of Erikson's thought. However, it is not an insight that can be obtained alone from the emphasis upon how we are effected by history as that emphasis is elaborated in philosophical hermeneutics. Rather a broader and more elaborated view of individual life history, including the prehistory described in this conclusion, is needed to supplement Gadamer's thesis of historical situatedness and his conception of *wirkungsgeschichtliches Bewusstsein*.

There are, then, two options for philosophical hermeneutics concerning the possibility and the desirability of a hermeneutics of life history. The first of these options is to continue to treat it as an overshadowed, if not antagonistic, topic. Essential to this option is the polemical comparison of historical belongingness with personal achievement and the belief that it is necessary to make this comparison in order to give historical situatedness its due importance. It treats one conception of consciousness, *wirkungsgeschichtliches Bewusstsein* of course, as of paramount importance and emphasizes within this consciousness the role of limitation and human finitude. This consciousness supports and is supported by the happening structure of play and other hermeneutical events. For this option the focus on subjectivity is a "distorting mirror" and play is an event "more than" it is an action.

The second option is, of course, the one that I have urged for adoption. This option treats individual life history as an important subject in its own right and argues for an essential role for personal achievement within the consideration of that history. Important to this option is a concern for preservation within life history that values childhood in a manner similar to tradition in an "achievement history" of the individual and the belief in the complementarity between historical belongingness and personal achievement. It proposes another conception of consciousness, the consciousness of having been enabled, as a necessary and useful complement to historically effected consciousness and emphasizes within this consciousness the role of enablement and the belief in individual capability. This consciousness supports and is supported by an "action structure" of childhood play, adolescent aspiration, adult work, and the reasons of old age. For this option the operative metaphor is that of a dynamic balance— between individual life history and history/tradition, between personal achievement and historical belonging-ness, between the consciousness of having been enabled and historically effected consciousness, and, now in the conclusion, between the "preachievements" and the "prejudices" of the individual.

For the second option to become a viable option and the language of balance to be more than a figure of speech, an important sense of enablement and its aspects of agency, will, and purpose has to be acknowl-edged from within the context of philosophical herme-neutics. If this sense is not acknowledged in its importance, then the rhetorical thrust against individual self-awareness and subjectivity will persist and philo-sophical hermeneutics will continue to be perceived as indifferent, if not hostile, to the subject of personal achievement. If, on the other hand, an important sense of enablement is recognized, then the different concerns that Gadamer and Erikson have for preserva-tion—namely, in the prejudices of our historical connectedness to tradition and in the preachievements of the playfulness of childhood play—can be seen not just as curious coincidences, but rather as indices of the contributions that can be made by philosophical herme-neutics to the subject of life history and by a hermeneu-tically sympathetic treatment of personal achievement to the rhetoric of philosophical hermeneutics. I have sought to indicate what these mutual contributions are without belittling the subject matter of personal achieve-ment or, conversely, denying the significance of histor-ical belongingness.

Notes

Introduction

[1]For a list of abbreviations used both in the text and in the footnotes, see the list of abbreviations on pp. xiii–xv.

[2]The transition from philosophies of consciousness to philosophies of language and communication is one that has occurred over a broad range of philosophical approaches and has been commented upon favorably, if a very imprecise terminology be pardoned, by Gadamer's "friends" and "foes" alike. See *Philosophy and the Mirror of Nature* by Richard Rorty (Princeton: Princeton University Press, 1979), *Reflexion und Diskurs: Fragen einer Logik der Philosophie* by Herbert Schnädelbach (Frankfurt: Suhrkamp, 1977), *Die Transformation der Philosophie* by Karl Otto Apel (Frankfurt: Suhrkamp, 1971), and Habermas's *PDM*.

[3]The other translations for *wirkungsgeschichtliches Bewusstsein* are taken from, respectively, Richard E. Palmer, *Hermeneutics* (Evanston: Northwestern University Press, 1969), p. 191, and David Hoy, *The Critical Circle* (Berkeley: University of California Press, 1978), p. 63.

[4]I am thankful to Donald G. Marshall and Joel C. Weinsheimer, the editors of the new translation, for communicating to me about this matter. Their endeavor to provide a new translation of *Truth and Method* is both laudatory and necessary. Inasmuch as, however, their new translation was not available to me, I did encounter many translation difficulties. A good number of citations are as translated in the first edition; but whenever there were conflicts with translations offered by Weinsheimer in GH or by David Linge in his Introduction to PH, their translations were preferred. In certain instances I also made my own modifications and these modifications are noted in the references. Thus in the references the page numbers are to where the passage appears in the first edition of T&M, but the passages themselves are not always cited as translated in that edition.

[5]It is quite difficult to obtain a precise reading of the effects of failing to recognize our belongingness to history. In general, Gadamer appears to argue that we belong to history "beyond our willing and doing." However, there are also passages in T&M, such as on p. 322, where it is said of the advocate of objective method that "he thereby detaches himself from the continuing action of tradition, in which he himself has his historical reality." Probably the best expression of the effect of being unaware of

tradition appears on pp. 48–49 of RB: "as finite beings, we already find ourselves within certain traditions, irrespective of whether we are aware of them or whether we deceive ourselves into believing we can start anew. For our attitude does nothing to change the power that tradition exercises over us. But it makes a difference whether we face up to the traditions in which we live along with the possibilities they offer for the future, or whether we manage to convince ourselves that we can turn away from the future into which we are already moving and program ourselves afresh."

[6]Bruner's distinction gains in plausibility from the fact that Erikson makes a very similar distinction with respect to Freud on p. 40 of LHHM. There Erikson distinguishes between Freud's "scientism" and his "literary and phenomenological approach."

Chapter 1

[1]Albert Hofstadter, Introduction to *Poetry, Language, Thought* (New York: Harper & Row, 1971), xix–xx. The whole Introduction is a helpful exposition of some of the difficulties in translating the later Heidegger.

[2]Gadamer originally considered giving *Wahrheit und Methode* the title *Geschehen und Verstehen* ("event and understanding"), but declined to do so because of pressure from the publisher.

[3]See chap. 4 of Grondin's HW for a more thorough discussion of this important theme, and above all for the relationship of Gadamer's discussion of the truth of the work of art to Heidegger's essay on the origin of the work of art.

[4]Material from this paragraph has been taken and adapted from an earlier essay of mine, "Philosophical Hermeneutics and the Conflict of Ontologies," *International Philosophical Quarterly*, 24 (September 1984), pp. 293–94.

[5]Otto Pöggeler, "Being as Appropriation," *Philosophy Today*, 19 (Summer 1975), p. 174.

Chapter 2

[1]This study will not take up the issue of Hegel's own understanding of *Bildung*, a topic of great proportions and many different dimensions in its own right. In addition, the accuracy of both Gadamer's and Habermas's interpretations of Hegel will not be contested nor will the fairness or persuasiveness of their criticisms of Hegel be probed. Instead the focus will be solely upon the Gadamer/Habermas comparison made possible by their different Hegel interpretations.

I do want to point out, however, a study on the subject of Hegel's philosophy of *Bildung: The Spirit and Its Letter: Traces of Rhetoric in Hegel's*

Philosophy of Bildung, by John H. Smith (Ithaca: Cornell University Press, 1988), which is quite relevant to both the themes of this chapter and the general thesis of the whole book. Smith analyzes the role of tradition and the largely unacknowledged debt to rhetoric in Hegel's philosophy of *Bildung* in a way that exhibits great commonality with Gadamer's interpretation of Hegel and the general themes of philosophical hermeneutics. Smith writes concerning the role of rhetoric and of hermeneutical interpretation for Hegel: "He goes on to say of the Spirit: 'its depth [is] only as deep as it allows itself to expand and lose itself in its interpretation or exegesis (*Auslegung*)' (p. 18 [*Phenomenology*]). This statement implies that part of the Spirit's power of expression, part of its *Bildung*, arises from a power of interpretation, explication, application, and self-loss in its object. It implies further an underlying logic by which self-loss in some Other can lead to better self-expression. . . . The unfolding of the Spirit involves . . . a hermeneutical impulse to interpret, an impulse that presumes and philosophically reformulates a temporal-historical component of rhetorical *Bildung*" (p. 14). At the same time, however, that Smith expresses and develops this "rhetorico-hermeneutical" aspect of *Bildung*, he also gives equal emphasis to a critical and personal achievement aspect of *Bildung*. See the footnote on this point in chapter 5, below.

[2]Smith points out that while Hegel clearly was devoted to the classics and traditional rhetoric, he also was interested in, and sought as a gymnasium director to incorporate, Enlightenment pedagogical theories as well (pp. 84–88).

[3]Concerning the fairness of this criticism, see Grondin's discussion in HW, pp. 58ff. His conclusion is that "Gadamer's way—as opposed to his own self-understanding—differs therefore little from that of Hegel" (HW, 59).

[4]See, for example, Gadamer's discussion on pp. 122–24 of PH.

[5]That is, at the stage of his thought that is being examined in this chapter. Later the ties to idealism are much less strong, as comments on Habermas's TCA in chapter 5, below, make clear. See also PDM, pp. 299–301.

[6]The other is, of course, Karl Marx. Already in the essay on Hegel, Habermas writes of Marx, "Thus without any knowledge of the Jena manuscripts, Marx had rediscovered that interconnection between labor and interaction" (T&P, 168). In K&HI, this interconnection is more extensively clarified: "Marx takes the dialectic of the moral life, which operates on the basis of social labor, as the law of motion of a defined conflict between definite parties. The conflict is always about the organization of the appropriation of socially created products, while the conflicting parties are determined by their position in the process of production, that is as classes. As the movement of class antagonism, the dialectic of the moral life is linked to the development of social labor" (K&HI, 57). However, in the Hegel essay Marx is already criticized, as he

will later be criticized in K&HI: "Marx does not actually explicate the interrelationship of interaction and labor, but instead, under the unspecific title of social praxis, reduces the one to the other, namely: communicative action to instrumental action" (T&P, 168–69).

⁷The date of publication of S&R is two years later than the date of publication of K&HI. However, in the preface to K&HI, Habermas clearly acknowledges his indebtedness to Lorenzer: "I owe thanks to Alfred Lorenzer, who gave me access to the manuscript of his study of the methodological role of understanding in psychoanalysis." Other important works from Lorenzer (all from Suhrkamp) include: *Kritik des psychoanalytischen Symbolbegriffs; Zur Begründung einer materialistischen Sozialisationstheorie; Über den Gegenstand der Psychoanalyses oder: Sprache und Interaktion*; and *Die Wahrheit der psychoanalytischen Erkenntnis.*

⁸That is, returned to being a symbol as opposed to being a cliché (see the following pages for an elucidation of the term "cliché").

⁹"Self-reflection is not a solitary movement; it is tied to the intersubjectivity of linguistic communication with an other. In the end, self-consciousness is constituted only on the basis of mutual recognition" (K&HI, 344–45n).

¹⁰The relating of Fichte and Freud in such a close fashion is also reflected in a quotation from Arnold Gehlen: "Both of the most important and consequential philosophical discoveries of the last two centuries go back to Fichte. They are the dialectical method of thought and the here discussed Fichtean formula of the 'lost freedom,' of the alienation and overpoweringness of our own products. In psychological application this Fichtean formula has become popular throughout the world without anyone having really noticed: in Freud." (In "Über die Geburt der Freiheit aus der Entfremdung," *Studien zur Anthropologie und Soziologie* (Neuwied, 1963), p. 234; translation is my own.)

Chapter 3

¹The entire sentence reads: "Das Bewusstsein der Bedingtheit hebt die Bedingtheit selbst keineswegs auf" (W&M, 424).

²Compare the following commentary from Grondin (made about *both* Hegel and Gadamer!): "The subjects are not so much the movers as the moved. They participate in history, without being able to grasp beyond it. . . . The individuals are in this way not the true 'subject' of history. . . . Through the *yielding (Ausweichen)* of the subject is found, so to say, another subject" (HW, 58; my emphasis).

³In a footnote on p. 451 of IC, Geertz writes: "All this coupling of the occidental great with the oriental lowly will doubtlessly disturb certain sorts of aestheticians as the earlier efforts of anthropologists to speak of Christianity and totemism in the same breath disturbed certain sorts of theologians. . . . In any case, the attempt to deprovincialize the concept of

art is but part of the general anthropological conspiracy to deprovincialize all important social concepts—marriage, religion, law, rationality—and though this is a threat to aesthetic theories which regard certain works of art as beyond the reach of sociological analysis, it is no threat to the conviction, for which Robert Graves claims to have been reprimanded at his Cambridge tripos, that some poems are better than others."

[4]Further comment on the exact wording of MacIntyre's claim about co-authorship may be called for. MacIntyre is claiming that we are never more (and sometimes less) than co-authors against a context of individualistic liberal thought. Hence in some ways the circumstances of his claim are quite similar to Gadamer's claims against the Enlightenment. However, whereas Gadamer limits subjectivity so much as to call it a distorting mirror, MacIntyre chooses to write of co-authorship instead.

Chapter 4

[1]Erikson proliferates, so to speak, charts about the life cycle or about factors correlated with the life cycle. Thus the cycle of psychosocial crises is correlated with schedules of psychosocial modalities, of a changing radius of significant social relationships, of related elements of the social order, with a table of ethical virtues, and still other factors. The broadest example of a chart that I have been able to find is on pp. 32–33 of LCC (see opposite). The range of subject matters under each stage leads Bruner to call each of them "genres."

[2]The translation of this passage is partially from Thomas McCarthy, CTJH, pp. 341–42, and partially my own. Other quoted passages from EI are my translations as are the quoted passages from ZRHM, MH, VET, KK, and ZLS.

[3]The other possibility is that the subjects involved may take part in strategic action no longer directed toward consensus. For the concept of strategic action, see the important comments in CTJH, pp. 24–26.

[4]Habermas's most recent comments on the theme of social identity have occurred not within a theoretical context, but the quite different context of the *Historikerstreit*. For a collection of essays associated with this controversy, see *Historikerstreit. Die Dokumentation der Kontroverse um die Einzigartigkeit der nationalsozialistischen Judenvernichtung* (Munich: Piper, 1987). Probably the most significant contribution by Habermas on the theme of identity does not, however, appear in that collection or in the translated essays from the collection in number 44 of *New German Critique*. That contribution, "Geschichtsbewusstsein und posttraditionelle Identität," appears in volume 6 of *Kleine politische Schriften* (Frankfurt: Suhrkamp, 1987) and is commented upon by Charles S. Maier in his book, *The Unmasterable Past. History, Holocaust, and German National Identity* (Cambridge: Harvard University Press, 1988), on pp. 151–54.

Stages	A Psychosexual Stages and Modes	B Psychosocial Crises	C Radius of Significant Relations	D Basic Strengths	E Core-Pathology Basic Antipathies	F Related Principles of Social Order	G Binding Ritualizations	H Ritualism
I Infancy	Oral-Respiratory, Sensory-Kinesthetic (Incorporative Modes)	Basic Trust vs. Basic Mistrust	Maternal Person	Hope	Withdrawal	Cosmic Order	Numinous	Idolism
II Early Childhood	Anal-Urethral, Muscular (Retentive-Eliminative)	Autonomy vs. Shame, Doubt	Parental Persons	Will	Compulsion	"Law and Order"	Judicious	Legalism
III Play Age	Infantile-Genital, Locomotor (Intrusive, Inclusive)	Initiative vs. Guilt	Basic Family	Purpose	Inhibition	Ideal Prototypes	Dramatic	Moralism
IV School Age	"Latency"	Industry vs. Inferiority	"Neighborhood," School	Competence	Inertia	Technological Order	Formal (Technical)	Formalism
V Adolescence	Puberty	Identity vs. Identity Confusion	Peer Groups and Outgroups; Models of Leadership	Fidelity	Repudiation	Ideological Worldview	Ideological	Totalism
VI Young Adulthood	Genitality	Intimacy vs. Isolation	Partners in friendship, sex, competition, cooperation	Love	Exclusivity	Patterns of Cooperation and Competition	Affiliative	Elitism
VII Adulthood	(Procreativity)	Generativity vs. Stagnation	Divided Labor and shared household	Care	Rejectivity	Currents of Education and Tradition	Generational	Authoritism
VIII Old Age	(Generalization of Sensual Modes)	Integrity vs. Despair	"Mankind" "My Kind"	Wisdom	Disdain	Wisdom	Philosophical	Dogmatism

[5]The word "environment" is used in this quotation to refer to the specifically human, psychosocial environment in contrast to a "pseudo-biological" conception of the term.

[6]For some of the important historical changes that have occurred in the process of identity formation, see Roy F. Baumeister, *Identity: Cultural Change and the Struggle for Self* (Oxford: Oxford University Press, 1986), chapters 2–6. Baumeister's book offers very good background from history, sociology, and literary criticism concerning the concept of identity.

[7]Jerome Bruner writes that "social critics found his psychological rendering of the Marxist idea of alienation—the famous 'identity crisis'—a less pessimistic way of thinking about dropouts and delinquents" (AA, 8).

[8]Erikson's conception of ideology is commented upon favorably by Paul Ricoeur in I&U and also related by him to the conception of ideology of Clifford Geertz. Ricoeur originally intended to devote an entire lecture to Erikson in his lecture series that became I&U, but later only included references to Erikson in his lecture on Geertz.

[9]Alan Roland voices this suspicion on p. 314 of his book, *In Search of Self in India and Japan: Toward a Cross-Cultural Psychology* (Princeton: Princeton University Press):

> Erik Erikson interrelates social, cultural, and historical dimensions with the varied needs and challenges of the psychosocial dimensions of the development throughout the life cycle, as he has systematically elaborated these in his developmental schema. There is much to commend in this approach. The only problem is that in cross-cultural and psychohistorical interdisciplinary work in India and Japan it doesn't fully work. The tightly organized sections don't fit together.
>
> Why? Because Erikson systematized and universalized a developmental schema that is completely based on the data of Western personality. Strivings for autonomy and initiative in young children, or the identity crises, moratoria, and syntheses of adolescence and young adulthood may be central to American, and even Western development, but they certainly are not to Indian and Japanese development. His schema not only emphasizes what is not central to their development, but completely omits what is paramount—such as the child's reactions to the active encouragement of dependency needs in the earlier phases of childhood, and the child's negotiation of the severe crackdown on behavior in familial hierarchical relationships from ages four or five through adolescence. In effect, Erikson has kept his section of the pot too intact to fit in with the cultural, social, and historical dimensions of these societies. In psychohistorical and cross-cultural work in India and Japan, the psychological section has to be considerably modified in order to interrelate with other dimensions of reality.

It is important to note that, although Roland favors "de-Westernizing the specific content" of Erikson's schema, it is not necessarily to favor a larger, more universal contextualization of the data, but rather "a new contextualization based on the data of Indians and Japanese" (p. 320).

Chapter 5

[1]Erikson is, of course, not the only prominent figure to have researched into the phenomenon of childhood play. He does, however, perhaps go the furthest, as will be seen in this chapter, in the employment of "big words" for "wordless play" and for this reason above all he is compared with Gadamer. For two of the classic studies on childhood play and its social, cognitive, and moral significance, see George Herbert Mead, *Mind, Self, and Society* (Chicago: University of Chicago Press, 1934), and Jean Piaget, *The Moral Judgment of the Child* (New York: Free Press, 1965). For perhaps the most famous classic philosophical study of play, see Johan Huizinga, *Homo Ludens* (London: Routledge and Kegan Paul, 1949).

[2]Compare the following quote on play and the work of art from the otherwise excellent book by Grondin on Gadamer: "Thereby is the play not to be seen as something playful, childish or diversionary, but as the most serious thing. Only he who seriously plays really plays. Otherwise the play is ruined" (HW, 104). Erikson is claiming, I believe, that only he or she who really plays seriously works and otherwise the work is ruined.

[3]See, for example, chapter 18, "Of the Subject Who Is Supposed To Know, of the First Dyad, and of the Good," in *The Four Fundamental Concepts of Psychoanalysis* (New York: Norton, 1978), pp. 230–43.

[4]See Bruner's interesting discussion on this subject in AA.

[5]Other testimonies to the power of childhood play appear in the remarkable *Children and Play in the Holocaust* by George Eisen (Amherst: University of Massachusetts Press, 1988). Compare Robert's block construction with the pebble game of a wartime ghetto boy that reenacts death and at the same time expresses the struggle to survive: "Nothing could express the anguish and pain of the Holocaust more painfully and literally than the following enactment of a tragedy beyond human scale— the capsulation of the Holocaust in the child's game. A teacher in the Lodz ghetto noticed a one-sided discussion between a little boy, whose whole family was already deported, and a five-year-old girl. 'He was dawdling and talking loudly to himself, . . .' she wrote about the scene. 'One hand was full of small stones':

> At first the boy dropped three small stones. They hit the ground with a slight sound, then two more, followed by another three. Next the little boy quickly closed his fist. In his lively eyes the shiny black pupils stopped their race for a moment. . . . 'Nine brothers like these stones we were once, all close together. Then came the first deportation and three of the brothers didn't return, two were shot at the barbed wire fences and three died of hunger. Can you guess how many brother-stones are still left in my hand?" [p. 116]

Compare also the rag doll play of the five-year-old Ettie on p. 76.

[6]Gadamer has given another example of a description of play in RB that does refer to the play of a child who is caught up in how many times it can bounce a ball on the ground. Of this play, and of similar play by adults, Gadamer writes: "In this form of nonpurposive activity, it is reason

itself that sets the rules. . . . The end pursued is certainly a nonpurposive activity, but this activity is intended. It is what the play intends. In this fashion we actually intend something with effort, ambition, and profound commitment. . . . The function of the representation of play is ultimately to establish, not just any movement whatsoever, but rather the movement of play determined in a specific way" (RB, 23). This example of play is probably more complementary with Erikson's description of play than the discussion of play in T&M. It is, however, following Erikson's taxonomy, a far better example of the "technical mastery of toys and *things*" than of "mastering *experience*," which is of course Erikson's primary interest in describing Robert's play and even the play of the eighteen-month-old toddler.

[7]Dieter Misgeld, "Critical Theory and Hermeneutics: The Debate between Habermas and Gadamer," *On Critical Theory*, John O'Neill, ed. (New York: Seabury), p. 178.

[8]It is interesting to compare what Erikson writes about meaning an affect with John H. Smith's analysis in his earlier mentioned study of Hegel's "taking a position." Concerning Hegel's period in Bern, Smith writes: "We must ask what model—or which one possible model—Hegel might have had of *Bildung*. The *form* of the fragments makes clear that he was working with a model of *Bildung* which emphasized that process by which the young writer must paradoxically work his way to independence through imitation" (119). And Hegel's personal *Bildung* in Jena is depicted in terms that are even more in accord with the general thesis of this study concerning the balancing of personal achievement with the historical tradition: "Hegel enters the public sphere. . . . His *Bildung* shifts from imitations and translations to an act of taking a position. Taking a position involves simultaneously differentiating oneself from others critically . . . and synthesizing various ideas into one's own stance. . . . If in Bern and Frankfurt he worked through the age-old rhetorico-hermeneutical paradox of how to attain individuality by means of imitative appropriation of general principals, in Jena he confronts the paradox of how to differentiate himself from others without becoming just one more different position" (140–41).

[9]The focus on the great young rebel and the young man in these quoted passages may provide the appropriate occasion to note an observation from Carol Gilligan in her article, "Woman's Place in Man's Life Cycle," that "it turns out to be the male child—the coming generation of men like George Bernard Shaw, William James, Martin Luther, and Mahatma Gandhi—who provide Erikson with his most vivid illustrations" (WP, 63). The focus on the highly individuated identity of these men has the consequence, according to Gilligan, that separation is valued more highly than attachment in the process of development so that many of the important contributions of women are overlooked: "Erikson . . . attempts to grapple with this problem of integration. But when he charts a developmental path where the sole precursor to the intimacy of adult love

and the generativity of adult work and relationships is the trust established in infancy, and where all intervening experience is marked as steps toward autonomy and independence, then separation itself becomes the model and the measure of growth. Though Erikson observes that, for women, identity has as much to do with intimacy as with separation, this observation is not integrated into his developmental chart" (DV, 98). In emphasizing the importance of attachment, Gilligan is, under my interpretation, advancing a very important criticism of the model of separation and union primarily in respect to the original sense of "balance" rather than to the sense advocated here between belongingness and achievement. I may, however, be mistaken in my interpretation.

[10]Here it may be useful to compare my interpretation of Erikson and Gadamer with an interesting critical discussion of Gadamer by Grondin. Grondin writes of the relationship of history and truth to the subject in Gadamer: "Truth is then an effective historical happening in which we participate. This inexact and misleading way of speaking would however gain in credibility, if the weightings would be more carefully distributed. The statements of Gadamer lead often to placing the subject as a tiny element in the play of effective history. Doubtless the subject does not let itself be thought on the other side of (*jenseits*) effective history. Nonetheless it would be perhaps more advisable in reference to the happening of truth to speak of a play *between* effective history *and* the subject. . . . The hermeneutic event of truth lies in the medial interplay of both components" (HW, 168–69). The phrase "medial interplay" refers to the attempt by Gadamer to explain the activity of the subject in neither active nor passive voice: "Gadamer sees the necessity to assign both aspects [the self and the substance of history] the right place in order to give precedence to a new subjectivity under the catchword 'openness' that replaces Heidegger's *Gelassenheit*. The interplay of both a passive and an active element should be produced. The 'activity' which brings forth the happening of truth lets itself be appropriately depicted in neither an active nor a passive verb form. Gadamer proposes a middle line, so to say, in that he attempts to bring both aspects into a *medial* genus" (HW, 168). Under my interpretation, Erikson is doing much the same thing in his analysis of young Luther—not, however, in order to limit and change the notion of subjectivity, but rather to balance it with tradition and social structure as the above quote indicates.

Chapter 6

[1]This comparison between different disproportions was suggested to me by a discussion by Karl Löwith of Goethe's essay "Shakespeare und kein Ende" on p. 198 of *From Hegel to Nietzsche: The Revolution in Nineteenth-century Thought* (trans. David E. Green, New York: Holt, Rinehart and Winston, 1964):

> In the literature of the ancients, the disproportion between what
> man *should* do and what he accomplishes is dominant; in that of the
> moderns, it is the disproportion between what he *wills* to do and
> what he accomplishes. What a man should do is imposed upon a
> man from without, what he wills to do he imposes upon himself. In
> the one case, all appears to be destiny, in the other freedom.

I am of course aware that Gadamer's concern is not with destiny, but I do
feel that "all appears to be" tradition for him and am seeking an
equilibrium similar to both that which Goethe finds in Shakespeare and
that which Löwith also finds in Goethe.

[2]It would be an interesting exercise to compare this notion of
"automatic recourse" with the quite different notion of "being taken up in"
(*Eingenommensein*) in Gadamer's description of play. Being caught up in the
event can obviously have both positive and negative connotations. See also
descriptions of how participants are "caught up in" activities as disparate as
rock climbing and rock music in *Beyond Boredom and Anxiety* by Mihalyi
Csikszentmihalyi (San Francisco: Jossey-Bass Publishers, 1975).

[3]It is to be noted that I am employing the character of Isak Borg to
present ideas about Erikson's conception of final appropriation in
conjunction with his notion of a generativity crisis. If the process of final
appropriation is considered by itself, then its emphasis upon the
acceptance of death can occasion critical response. Ian Craib, for example,
objects against Erikson:

> I am also suspicious about what he has to say about integrity and the
> acceptance of death. His conception of integrity seems to miss the
> experience which most of us have of real internal conflict, real
> inadequacies and real damage, which can become a painful part of
> our wholeness. I can think of one example from my own practice: a
> man in his fifties who has managed to mourn his wasted years, but
> feels pleased with his children and wife, and faces the future
> knowing that he will probably continue to suffer panic attacks and
> depressions that threaten to be crippling, but that he can still
> manage them sufficiently well to start thinking again about possible
> career ambitions. This seems to me to involve an integrity that
> includes damage and conflict and pain and depression, as much as
> the sense of peace that Erikson implies. [P&ST, 84]

Craib's point is well taken, but I am not sure that Erikson's sense of peace
necessarily precludes the painful recognition of "the loss of friends, the
loss of a future, and the fight against death, despair and fear" (P&ST, 85).
Indeed the very fact that final appropriation and a discussion of
generativity crisis can be conjoined speaks against such an implication.

[4]Carol Gilligan has this comment to make about both *Wild Strawberries*
and Erikson's commentary to it: "Erikson, defining Marianne's role in
breaking the cycle of repetition that had extended across generations a
cold loneliness 'more frightening than death itself,' identifies the 'dominant
determination to care' in this 'quiet, independent girl with her naked,

observant eyes.' Yet in tracing the development of the virtue of care, which he views as the strength of adult life, he turns repeatedly to the lives of men. Since in life-cycle theory, as in the film, Marianne's story remains untold, it is never clear how she came to see what she sees or to know what she knows" (DV, 107).

[5]"Unconscious" in the meaning of "not conscious" and not as referring to the unconscious of Freud's topological model. If reference had to be made to this model, it would probably have to be called "preconscious." However, my belief is that Erikson would resist having to be put between these characterizations.

[6]Compare the similar ideas of vision and trust expressed in a speech by Margaret Cornelia Morgan Lawrence:

> Even the newborn sees her image reflected by the mirror of the mother's, father's, or caregiver's face. On the other side of the mirror, the nonreflecting, see-through side, lie generations of related images with a long history, representing the cultures of which they are a part, and their traditions. These images carry their religious traditions and their mother tongues as well. They find their end point in the mother's own image. The infant fastens her attention on the mother's face, absorbing the image which becomes her own. There is mutural engagement of the two images, mother's and daughter's. There is vitality that flows between the two images and the inner lives they represent. It is through this flow that the value of each is confirmed.

The excerpt appears on p. 312 of a moving biography of Lawrence by her daughter, Sara Lawrence Lightfoot: *Balm in Gilead* (Reading: Addison-Wesley, 1988).

[7]Compare Bruner: "I would have thought a formulation as sweeping as this one would force a major revision in psychoanalytic theory—though not so much in practice. For psychoanalysis is . . . considerably closer to Erikson's position in practice than in what it preaches" (AA, 13).

Selected Bibliography

Bergman, Ingmar. *Four Screenplays of Ingmar Bergman*. New York: Simon and Shuster, 1960.

Browning, Donald. *Generative Man: Psychoanalytic Perspectives*. New York: Dell, 1975.

Bruner, Jerome. "The Artist as Analyst." *The New York Review of Books*, 34, no. 19 (December 3, 1987), 8–13.

Coles, Robert. *Erik H. Erikson: The Growth of His Work*. Boston: Little, Brown, 1970.

Craib, Ian. *Psychoanalysis and Social Theory: The Limits of Sociology*. London: Harvester Wheatsheaf, 1989.

Erikson, Erik. *Childhood and Society*. 2nd, enlarged ed. New York: Norton, 1963.

——. *Dimensions of a New Identity: The 1975 Jefferson Lectures*. New York: Norton, 1974.

——. *Gandhi's Truth*. New York: Norton, 1969.

——. *Identity and the Life Cycle*. New York: Norton, 1980.

——. *Identity: Youth and Crisis*. New York: Norton, 1968.

——. *Insight and Responsibility*. New York: Norton, 1965.

——. *The Life Cycle Completed*. New York: Norton, 1982.

——. *Life History and the Historical Moment*. New York: Norton, 1975.

——. "Reflections on Dr. Borg's Life Cycle." In *Adulthood: Collected Essays*. Erik Erikson, ed. New York: Norton, 1978. 1–31.

——. *Toys and Reasons: Stages in the Ritualization of Experience*. New York: Norton, 1977.

——. *A Way of Looking at Things*. Stephen Schlein, ed. New York: Norton, 1987.

——. *Young Man Luther: a Study in Psychoanalysis and History*. New York: Norton. Austen Riggs Center, Monograph no. 4, 1958.

Gadamer, Hans-Georg. *Hegel's Dialectic: Five Hermeneutical Studies*. P. Christopher Smith, trans. New Haven: Yale University Press, 1976.

——. *The Idea of the Good in Platonic-Aristotelian Philosophy*. P. Christopher Smith, trans. New Haven: Yale University Press, 1986.

BIBLIOGRAPHY

————. *Philosophical Hermeneutics*. David E. Linge, trans. and ed. Berkeley: University of California Press, 1976.

————. *Reason in the Age of Science*. Frederick G. Lawrence, trans. Cambridge: MIT Press, 1981.

————. *The Relevance of the Beautiful and Other Essays*. Nicholas Walker, trans. Robert Bernasconi, ed. Cambridge: Cambridge University Press, 1986.

————. "Replik." In *Hermeneutik und Ideologiekritik*. Frankfurt: Suhrkamp, 1971. 283–317.

————. *Truth and Method*. Garrett Barden and John Cumming, eds. New York: Seabury, 1975.

————. *Wahrheit und Methode: Grundzüge einer philosophischen Hermeneutik*. 3rd ed. Tübingen: J. C. B. Mohr (Paul Siebeck), 1972.

Geertz, Clifford. "Deep Play: Notes on the Balinese Cockfight." In *The Interpretation of Cultures*. New York: Basic Books, 1973. 412–53.

————. *Local Knowledge*. New York: Basic Books, 1983.

Gilligan, Carol. *In a Different Voice*. Cambridge: Harvard University Press, 1982.

————. "Woman's Place in Man's Life Cycle." In *Feminism and Methodology*. Sandra Harding, ed. Bloomington: Indiana University Press, 1987.

Grondin, Jean. *Hermeneutische Wahrheit? Zum Wahrheitsbegriff Hans-Georg Gadamers*. Königstein: Forum Academicum, 1982.

Habermas, Jürgen. *Communication and the Evolution of Society*. Thomas McCarthy, trans. and ed. Boston: Beacon, 1970.

————. *Die Entwicklung des Ich*. R. Döbert, J. Habermas, and C. Nunner-Winkler, eds. Cologne: Kiepenheuer & Witsch, 1977.

————. *Habermas: Autonomy & Solidarity*. Peter Dews, ed. London: Verso, 1986.

————. *Habermas: Critical Debates*. J.B. Thompson and David Held, eds. Cambridge: MIT Press, 1982.

————. *Knowledge and Human Interests*. J. J. Shapiro, trans. Boston: Beacon, 1971.

————. *Kultur und Kritik: Verstreuete Aufsätze*. Frankfurt: Suhrkamp, 1973.

————. *Moralbewusstsein und kommunikatives Handeln*. Frankfurt: Suhrkamp, 1983.

————. *The Philosophical Discourse of Modernity*. Frederick Lawrence, trans. Cambridge: MIT Press, 1987.

————. "On Social Identity." *Telos* 19 (1974). 91–103.

————. *The Theory of Communicative Action. Volume One. Reason and the Rationalization of Society*. Thomas McCarthy, trans. Boston: Beacon, 1984.

————. *The Theory of Communicative Action. Volume Two. Lifeworld and System: A Critique of Functionalist Reason*. Thomas McCarthy, trans. Boston: Beacon, 1987.

————. "Toward a Theory of Communicative Competence." In *Recent Sociology, no. 2.* Hans Peter Dreitzel, ed. New York: Macmillan, 1970. 115–48.

————. *Theory and Practice.* J. Viertel, trans. Boston: Beacon, 1973.

————. *Vorstudien und Ergänzungen zur Theorie des kommunikativen Handelns.* Frankfurt: Suhrkamp, 1984.

————. *Zur Logik der Sozialwissenschaften.* Frankfurt: Suhrkamp, 1970.

————. *Zur Rekonstruktion des Historischen Materialismus.* Frankfurt: Suhrkamp, 1976.

Ingram, David. *Habermas and the Dialectic of Reason.* New Haven: Yale University Press, 1987.

Lorenzer, Alfred. *Sprachzerstörung und Rekonstruktion.* Frankfurt: Suhrkamp, 1970.

MacIntyre, Alasdair. *After Virtue.* 2nd ed. Notre Dame: Notre Dame University Press, 1984.

McCarthy, Thomas. *The Critical Theory of Jürgen Habermas.* Cambridge: MIT Press, 1978.

Ricoeur, Paul. *The Conflict of Interpretations: Essays in Hermeneutics.* Don Ihde, ed. Evanston: Northwestern University Press, 1974.

————. *Freud and Philosophy: An Essay on Interpretation.* Denis Savage, trans. New Haven: Yale University Press, 1970.

————. *Hermeneutics and the Human Sciences: Essays on Language, Action and Interpretation.* John B. Thompson, trans. and ed. Cambridge: Cambridge University Press, 1981.

————. *Interpretation Theory: Discourse and the Surplus of Meaning.* Fort Worth: Texas Christian University Press, 1976.

————. *Lectures on Ideology and Utopia.* George H. Taylor, ed. New York: Columbia University Press, 1986.

Wachterhauser, Brice, ed. *Hermeneutics and Modern Philosophy.* Albany: SUNY Press, 1986.

Warnke, Georgia. *Gadamer: Hermeneutics, Tradition and Reason.* Oxford: Polity Press, 1987.

Weinsheimer, Joel C. *Gadamer's Hermeneutics: A Reading of Truth and Method.* New Haven: Yale University Press, 1985.

White, Stephen. "Habermas' Communicative Ethics and the Development of Moral Consciousness." *Philosophy and Social Criticism* 10, no. 2 (1984). 25–48.

————. *The Recent Work of Jürgen Habermas: Reason, Justice & Modernity.* Cambridge: Cambridge University Press, 1988.

Index

Absolute knowledge, objected to by Gadamer, 36

Absolute spirit, relation to objective spirit for Gadamer, 36–37

Action structure: complementarity with event structure, 109–10; emphasis upon capabilities and activities of player, 109; enabling aspect of, 6; of play, 6, 13, 16, 96–98, 107–10, 128, 135. *See also* Happening structure

Adolescence, 1, 70, 75–76, 103, 113–14, 125; as period of identity acquisition according to Erikson, 89–94; characterized by psychological moratorium, 89–90, 92, 103. *See also* Social play

Adulthood, 113, 125, 135; automatic recourse in, 113, 146n.2

Apel, Karl Otto, 136n.2

Appropriation (*Aneignung*), 6, 7, 53, 56, 96, 110, 127; as both belongingness and achievement, 58; Gadamer's conception of, 9, 15–16, 17–24; in psychoanalysis, 49, 52; Ricoeur's conception of, 9, 16, 24–27; Romantic conception of, 15, 26. *See also* Personal appropriation

Aristotle, 22, 38

Balance: between event of appropriation and act of personal appropriation, 68; between historical belongingness and personal achievement, 2, 54, 66–68, 135; between historically effected consciousness and the consciousness of having been enabled, 135; between life history and historical event, 112, 135; between personal and social identity, 11, 65–66, 90–91, 94; Habermas's concept of, 65–66; modified, 66–67, 68

Balinese cockfight: as a play, 63; as a paradigmatic human event, 63–64; deep play of, 62; described by Geertz, 60–65; disquietful effect of, 62–63; in regard to adolescent aspiration, 103–6, 108–9; sentimental education of, 54, 60, 61, 63, 104, 105; status war, 61–63

Basic trust (Erikson), 111, 120–21

Baumeister, Roy F., 142n.6

Bentham, Jeremy, 62

Bergman, Ingmar, 13, 65, 112, 116, 121–23; *Wild Strawberries*, 13, 112, 115–18, 119, 121, 122, 126. *See also Wild Strawberries*

Bildung (Education, Culture, Self-formation): Erikson's implicit account of, 98, 106–10; Gadamer's conception of, 6, 7, 10, 12, 30, 31–39, 52–57, 59–60, 96–98, 110, 127, 130; Hegel's philosophy of, 34–36, 137–38n.1, 144n.8; in Herder, 33; process of formation both of and by self, 64–65, 106–10

Bildungsprozess (Process of self-formation): Habermas's conception of, 10, 30–32, 52, 53–54, 60, 81; in Hegel, 40–41

Black Panther Movement, 93–94

Blake, William, 97

Borg, Dr. Isak. *See Wild Strawberries*